AF572187

Ballparks

Ball

arks

Robert von Goeben

MetroBooks

MetroBooks
An Imprint of Friedman/Fairfax Publishers

Library of Congress Cataloging-in-Publication Data
Von Goeben, Robert
Ballparks / Robert Von Goeben.
p. cm.
Includes bibliographical references (p.) and index.
ISBN 1-56799-923-9
1. Baseball fields—United States. 2. Baseball fields—Canada. 3. Stadiums—United States. 4. Stadiums—Canada. I. Title.
GV879.5 .H69 2000
796.357'06'873-dc21 99-049635

Editor: Ann Kirby
Art Director: Jeff Batzli
Designer: Joseph Rutt
Photography Editor: Chris Toliver
Production Manager: Camille Lee

Color separations by Bright Arts Graphics (S) Pte. Ltd.
Printed in Hong Kong by Midas Printing Limited

3 5 7 9 10 8 6 4 2
For bulk purchases and special sales, please contact:
Friedman/Fairfax Publishers
Attention: Sales Department
15 West 26th Street
New York, NY 10010
212/685-6610 FAX 212/685-1307

Visit our website:
www.metrobooks.com

DEDICATION

To my wife, Kathryn, whose constant companionship at the ballpark brings me endless inspiration, as well as the latest gossip from *Vanity Fair*.

ACKNOWLEDGMENTS

Many thanks to Staci Slaughter and the crew at Pacific Bell Park. Tip of the ball cap to Doug McConnell and Jeff Magid, two of the squarest guys to come out of the windy city, as well as the Roach clan from the Big Apple.

Special thanks to the following teams for their assistance: Baltimore Orioles, Boston Red Sox, Chicago White Sox, Chicago Cubs, Cleveland Indians, Colorado Rockies, Arizona Diamondbacks, Seattle Mariners, Detroit Tigers, Houston Astros, Los Angeles Dodgers, Montreal Expos, New York Yankees, San Francisco Giants, Texas Rangers

Extra special thanks to Cory Suppes, whose incredible web site *Ballparks by Munsey & Suppes* (http://www.ballparks.com) is a must for any sports nut.

CONTENTS

WRIGLEY FIELD
HOME OF
CHICAGO CUBS
GAMES START ONE THIRTY
NATIONAL LEAGUE CHAMPIONS
GATE 3
CHICAGO
Solvay Coke
COLLINS & WIESE COAL CO.
COLLINS & WIESE COAL CO.
COKE
COMFORT WITH ECONOMY

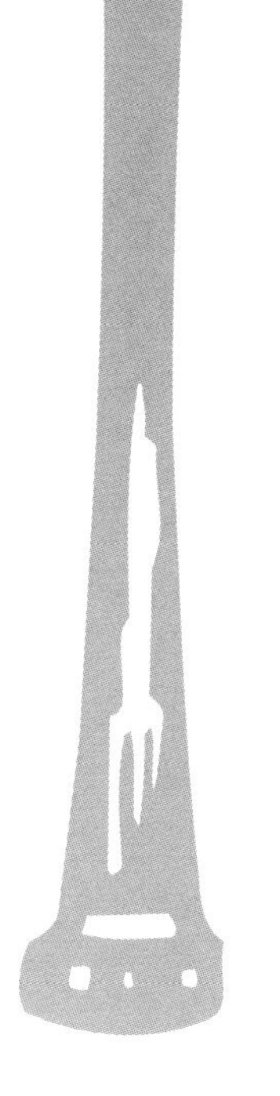

The Evolution of the Ballpark

A fan walks into a baseball park on a bright Saturday afternoon. He hands over his ticket at the gate, already hearing the growing din of the crowd inside. Once through the turnstile, he tugs on his home-team cap and marches to the concession stands. The stalwart patiently waits his turn and barks, "A dog and a beer." With goods in hand, our hero turns the corner to get his first glimpse of "big green," the majestic spread of grass that is the thrill of any serious ball-field connoisseur.

OPPOSITE: *Cubs fans mill around Chicago's Wrigley Field before the 1945 World Series against the Detroit Tigers.*

As he takes his seat, he thinks to himself that there's nothing finer than baseball under the right conditions.

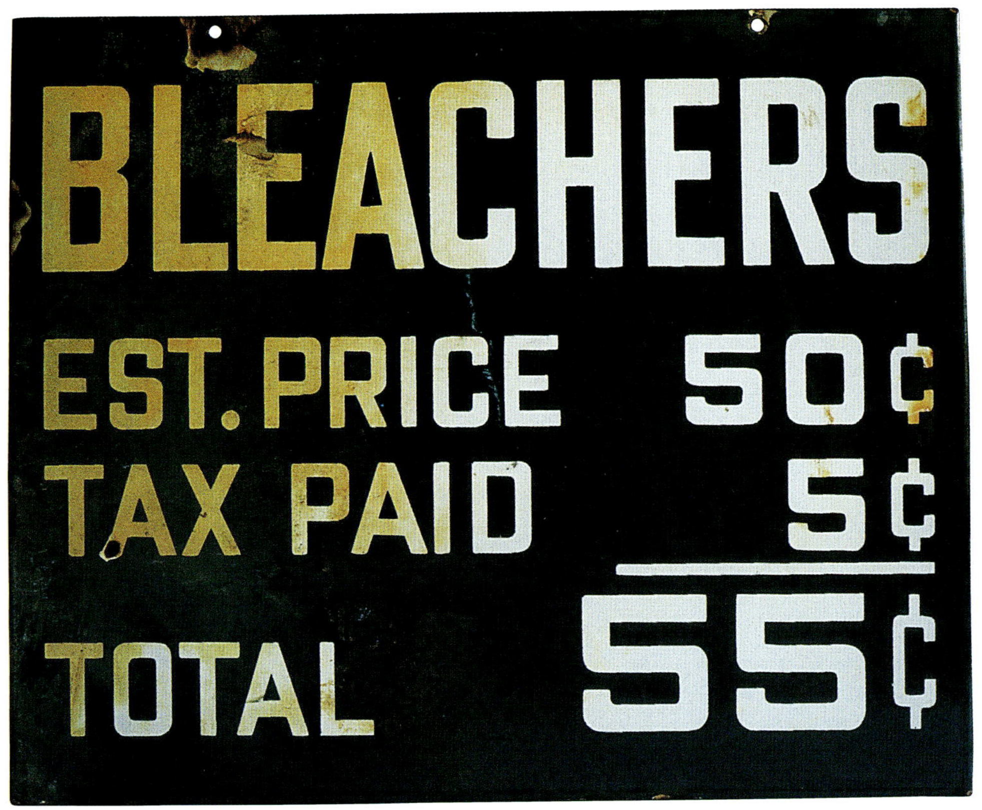

Baseball's original ball yards were humble confines, with prices to match.

He checks the sky for rain, and surveys his view of the field. Good visibility to the action at first, and the scoreboard is in good viewing range. He settles in and begins filling in his scorecard. When the national anthem is belted out, he dutifully rises. All is as it should be.

Let's face it. Baseball is a fussy sport.

The lure and romance of a baseball park stems from a simple, undeniable fact: you can't just toss baseball players and fans into any situation and expect them to like it. More than any other sport, baseball is invariably dependent on the environment in which it's played. If it rains, the game's canceled. Snow? Forget it. Even a strong wind will make any hitter complain about robbed home runs, and shivering fans complain about the lack of "baseball conditions." Baseball parks come under relentless scrutiny. A great ballpark is a treasure to the community and a joy to be in. A lousy ballpark just stinks.

The genetic code for a baseball park was created in the early twentieth century, when many of the legendary American ball fields were built. From 1910 to 1930, many of the timeless features we associate with baseball parks (brick facades, grass fields, manual scoreboards) were first emblazoned in our subconscious. And like the smell of hot dogs and the bark of a stadium vendor, these striking sensations so unique to baseball have established a permanent place in our collective memories. From Wrigley Field in Chicago to Fenway Park in Boston, these early-century ballparks soon set the standard for sandlots that, before the century was over, would be established, lost, and rediscovered. By 1950 the definition of a baseball park was set: a small urban park that offered an intimate setting, a real grass playing surface, and grand entrances featuring turn-of-the-century brick architecture. There's no denying it—when a ballpark is right, you know it. Any fan surveying the ivy-covered walls of Wrigley Field in Chicago is sure to proclaim, "Now *this* is a ballpark!"

Baseball is unique in many respects, but none more than this: there are no rules governing the overall size of the playing field. This unpredictable quality separates baseball from its major league brethren: differences among the various fields are unheard-of in such professional sports as football, basketball, soccer, and hockey. All four are played on rectangular grids whose dimensions are strictly dictated. Imagine the Packers arriving in San Francisco only to find the playing field ten yards longer! This militaristic rigidity brings with it consistent stadiums, and for many fans it's tough to tell one field from another. And while the rules of baseball do dictate the dimensions of the infield, the outfield and foul territory boundaries are fair game, allowing ballpark architects to personalize each field, with unpredictable (and sometimes amusing) consequences.

Many say the best baseball stadiums are "quirky," yet lovers of the classic ballpark could never imagine why a home run fence would be the same distance in right field as it is in left—that would just be too boring. Fan preference notwithstanding, let us not forget that the blueprint for a lopsided stadium came not out of eclectic design but economic reality. Baseball owners simply took advantage of the loose field requirements to squeeze a ballpark into the small amount of land available in early-twentieth-century urban centers. Football came of age after World War II, and benefited from a plethora of suburban land; baseball grew up in a time when the game, like most of the population, fought for space in America's cities.

Furthermore, baseball is much more of a small-theater art than the "rectangular" sports. While a play in football can unfold over fifty yards, the key elements of a baseball game occur over inches. Baseball minutiae like balks require acute focus, the kind of attention that can only be appreciated when you're close to the field. Hell, you can pack a hundred thousand people into a football game; the referees are even piped into the public address system. But if you've ever tried to read the signs from a third base coach, you know that baseball requires close quarters.

By the late 1950s, baseball had grown up and was ready to expand. Existing clubs moved to greener pastures out West, and new expansion teams were added. Somewhere along the line the geniuses of baseball began to view the old ballparks not as treasured monuments but as old relics. Not knowing what they had, postwar baseball owners rejected old ballparks for the suburban glitter (and potential profits) of monolithic "stadiums." Enter the modern era of baseball.

Baseball teams spent much of the 1960s and 1970s forsaking their historical homes and erecting gargantuan suburban monoliths, mistakenly thinking bigger parks meant bigger crowds. Like the teenager discarding his baseball-card collection, baseball owners rushed to the wrecking ball as park after classic park was bulldozed. First Ebbets Field in Brooklyn met the wrecking ball in 1960. A few years later, in 1964, Harlem's Polo Grounds met, coincidentally, with the very same wrecking ball. Forbes Field in Pittsburgh, Shibe Park in Philadelphia, Crosley Field in Cincinnati: gone, gone, gone. Hungry municipalities readily ponied up big cash in a quest for the biggest and best stadiums, desperate to avoid the brutal loss suffered by New York as both the Giants and the Dodgers packed up their bats and gloves and headed west.

The results speak for themselves. Baseball's classic parks were replaced by big concrete tombs, the best features of which were sterile symmetry and enormous capacities. These new monoliths were almost immediately hated by players and fans alike. Cinergy Field in Cincinnati, Three

Ernie Banks kicks up his heels outside Chicago's Wrigley Field after being elected to the Hall of Fame in 1977, his first year of eligibility. Banks spent nineteen years with the Cubs before retiring in 1971.

WELCOME TO
ORIOLE PARK AT CAMDEN YARDS
Bud
KING OF BEERS
Quality Gasolines
CROWN
CHEVY CHASE BANK
T. Rowe Price
FUJIFILM
WIZ

Baltimore's cozy Camden Yards, which went up in 1992, marked the beginning of a modern-day ballpark renaissance.

TOP: *The faithful watch from Coogan's Bluff as the Giants and Athletics battle in the 1905 World Series at the Polo Grounds in New York.* **BOTTOM:** *Shibe Park in Philadelphia, opened in 1909 and demolished in 1976, was the first baseball stadium built entirely of steel and concrete.*

Rivers Stadium in Pittsburgh, and Candlestick (later 3Com) Park in San Francisco were all designed with two things in mind: sharing the stadium with football teams and maximizing seat capacity. By the time stadiums had started ripping out the grass and putting in artificial turf in the '60s and '70s, ballparks had hit their nadir.

Come the 1980s, many aspects of the classic ballpark had gone by the wayside. Older baseball fans mourned the cozy confines of classic parks, and many younger fans grew up knowing nothing other than cold, sterile stadiums. Neither were satisfied, and the game's popularity plummeted. While the owners in luxury boxes may have lost touch with what made a great ballpark, the suffering fan never did. Try this some day: walk up to a fan in the stratospheric seats of Veterans Stadium in Philadelphia, look down at the glowing green of artificial turf, and ask him what a real baseball park is. Chances are he'll just look around and snort, "It ain't this."

By the time the century was coming to a close, the binge ended, and baseball teams woke up with large financial hangovers. Fans were universally rejecting the new breed of "concrete doughnut" stadiums. The era of baseball free agency had arrived, and invariably the teams that topped the standings were the teams that could get the butts in the seats, collect the cash, and lavish it on the pitcher with the 100-mph fastball, who was now commanding multiple millions per year.

The modern era officially ended in June 1989, when construction began on Camden Yards in Baltimore. The first baseball-only stadium to be built since Dodger Stadium in 1962, Camden Yards, with its brick architecture and downtown location, was a throwback to the parks of yesteryear. The strategy was simple: build a park that fans will enjoy, and they will flock there in droves. Next, use the increased revenue to buy better players; the team wins, more people come

to the stadium, and so on. Call it the ballpark formula of the 1990s; soon almost every team was trying to duplicate the recipe.

The end of the twentieth century will be remembered for a lot of things, but in the world of baseball there will be nothing more memorable than the slew of new heroes and old-fashioned ballparks. Just as Mark McGwire, Sammy Sosa, and Cal Ripken were ripping up the record books in the spirit of Ruth, Maris, and Gehrig, a new crop of retro ballparks brought us all back to the days of Ebbets Field and the Polo Grounds. From 1990 to 2000, more than a dozen new major league stadiums went up in the United States. Paying penance for the past, many hope these new fields will revitalize the economics of baseball and at the same time instill a brand of civic pride denied by the stadiums of the '60s and '70s.

To be fair, this race for new confines also has its drawbacks. Baseball is currently suffering through an intense "have–have not" phase.

ABOVE: *Best known for its unusual rock formation in centerfield, Edison Field has been the home of the Anaheim Angels since 1966.*

A vendor hawks souvenirs to fans in the nosebleed seats at The Coliseum in Oakland, CA.

WELCOME
Budweiser
400
375
330
OAKLAND
Athletics
1
13

Royals
Kauffman Stadium
AMERICAN LEAGUE
BLUE JAYS
ROYALS
BALL
STRIKE
OUT
AT BAT
Sprint
conoco
375
400
400

FAR LEFT: *Kauffman Stadium, home of the Kansas City Royals since 1973.* **LEFT:** *Warm-ups before the 1991 American League Championship Series at the Metrodome in Minneapolis, Minnesota.* **ABOVE:** *The hallowed halls of Yankee Stadium in New York, as seen from across the Harlem River.*

Granted, much of this inequity has to do with television revenue as well. But when you're a broke, losing team stuck with an outdated park and disgruntled fans, you understand that wanting a new ballpark is more than just being "fussy," it's keeping up with the Joneses—or more precisely, the Turners and the Murdochs (the media moguls who bought the Braves and the Dodgers, respectively).

But for the fans, the business side is an afterthought compared to the experience of being in a great ballpark. From Jacobs Field in Cleveland to Coors Field in Denver to Pacific Bell Park in San Francisco, these new parks evoke a uniform but simple public sentiment: the ballpark is once again a great place to be.

With this, we return to the fussy fan at the ballpark. The last innings of an afternoon game play out as long shadows make their way across the field. He looks down at his scorecard, now stained with mustard, and relives the past couple hours of his life. Relishing the beauty of the baseball diamond and admiring the elegant simplicity of the steel grandstands, he realizes they were pretty good hours.

San Diego's mammoth Qualcomm Stadium, which has a baseball capacity of more than 67,000.

SLICERIA
FITNESS
Taylor Made
COX

NEW YORK

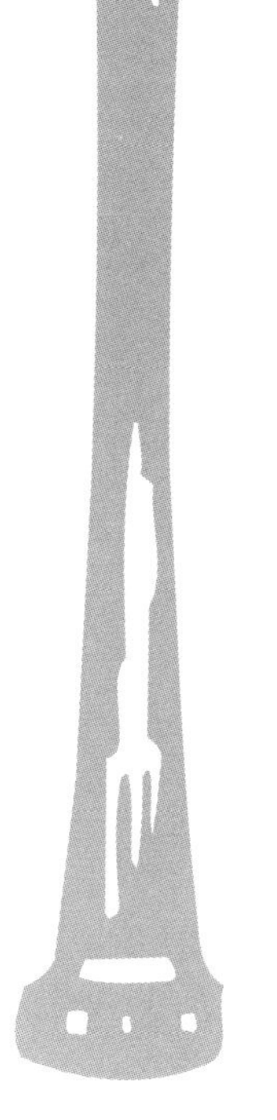

CHAPTER I

The Classic Era, 1900–1960

While ballparks quickly came of age in the first decade of the twentieth century, their humble beginnings bore little resemblance to the grand stadiums we know today. Baseball parks began as little more than fields, representative of the game's origins in the sport of cricket. In September 1845, a twenty-five-year-old shipping clerk named Alexander Cartwright formed the Knickerbocker Base Ball Club of New York, naming it after a volunteer fire company in which he had served. Cartwright began to fashion rules for a game based on cricket, but one that played much faster. On October 6, 1845, the first recorded game was played using Cartwright's new rules, which featured a diamond-shaped field. The historic

OPPOSITE: *New York Yankee Gene Woodling is greeted at the dugout after belting a homer in the 1953 World Series at Ebbets Field.*

Elysian Fields in Hoboken, New Jersey, considered the cradle of American baseball, circa 1866.

game lasted a scant three innings, but in that short time, a national pastime was born.

By most accounts, the first ball field popped up in New Jersey, which is ironic since the Garden State has never had a major league team in the modern era. The upstart New York Knickerbockers sought a playing ground for their new game, and landed just across the Hudson River in Hoboken. The team settled in a green pasture known as Elysian Fields. Named after a happy otherworld for heroes favored by the gods in Greek mythology, the site was perfect not only for its floral beauty, but for the nearby taverns. On June 19, 1846, the first recognized baseball game took place as the Knickerbockers and the New York Nine slugged it out. The New York Nine won handily, 23 to 1, and celebrated by feasting at the expense of the losers.

Baseball grew gradually from a clubby sport to organized contests, and eventually blossomed into a national obsession. By the first decade of the twentieth century, baseball had its National and American Leagues. In 1911 a new ball with a cork center was introduced, ending the so-called "dead ball era," and improving offense dramatically. As for the baseball diamond, it had progressed from fields to parks, then to stadiums. By 1909 it was obvious that the usual collection of wooden grandstands would not do. At the same time, improvements to construction techniques allowed for the building of more permanent structures.

The future of ballparks was sealed on April 12, 1909, when the magnificent Shibe Park opened in Philadelphia. The first ballpark constructed of concrete and steel, Shibe featured

Fans in "wildcat bleachers" enjoyed a free view of the 1914 World Series at Philadelphia's Shibe Park.

an opulent brick facade that became the trademark for many of the retro stadiums being built today. Shibe Park opened with an official capacity of 20,000, but more than 30,000 squeezed into the park on opening day, in keeping with early-century disregard for fire laws.

What started in Philadelphia soon created a ballpark frenzy across the United States. Between 1909 and 1923, new concrete-and-steel ballparks sprang up in Detroit, Boston, and Pittsburgh. Chicago got two new yards, and the greater New York City area saw the construction of a trio of classic halls: the Polo Grounds in Harlem, Ebbets Field in Brooklyn, and Yankee Stadium in the Bronx.

All of these classic parks had one thing in common: intimacy. While owners will inevitably want to cram as many people as possible into a ballpark, history has taught them that fans won't tolerate just any baseball environment. Throughout the twentieth century, ballparks have taken many different forms, from the casual fields of the 1800s to the 60,000-plus-capacity stadiums of the 1970s. But it was during this first decade of the 1900s that ball yards found their natural capacity, somewhere in the range of 40,000. For many intangible reasons, this capacity just feels right, and it's no coincidence that most of the memorable ballparks of the twentieth century—Ebbets field, Wrigley Field, Camden Yards, Jacobs Field—had capacities in this range.

From the elimination of the dead ball to the introduction of the designated hitter, many different factors have shaped the game of baseball. But it was these oddly shaped, brick-faced parks of the early 1900s that forever forged the field of play, and our image of the game.

The original Comiskey Park in Chicago, home of the world's first exploding scoreboard.

Comiskey Park

Chicago (1910–90)

Comiskey Park represented all that was industrial about Chicago's south side. Built in 1910 within spitting (and smelling) distance of Chicago's infamous slaughterhouses, Comiskey Park amounted to a no-frills workingman's ball yard. Born of humble blue-collar beginnings, Comiskey went on to have one of the most colorful histories of any American ballpark.

In 1910 owner Charles Comiskey found his White Sox doing pretty well, having bagged the pennant twice in the first decade of the century. Comiskey looked to move his team from their current home, a matchbox of a ball yard called South Side Park that held a scant 15,000 people, and brought in architect Zachary Taylor Davis (who later designed Wrigley Field) to design his new ballpark. But he also enlisted the help of White Sox spitballer and Hall of Famer Ed

Walsh, who helped design a decidedly large, pitcher-friendly park.

Comiskey Park was originally a double-decked grandstand that extended just beyond first and third bases, with single-deck stands extending to the foul poles and wooden bleachers in the outfield. Among its more proletarian features were view-blocking metal support beams, some directly in front of seats. The new park held 32,000 fans and cost $750,000 to build. Built on the site of a garbage dump, Comiskey was tossed up in just four and a half months, an amazing accomplishment considering the three- to four-year construction cycle of today's fields. In *Lost Ballparks,* author Lawrence S. Ritter recounts the story of how White Sox shortstop Luke Appling, smoothing the infield dirt before a game in the 1930s, met Comiskey's hasty construction foot-on. "I started digging with my spikes," Appling remembered, "and, lo and behold, I uncovered a blue-and-white teakettle. Quite an antique. The ground crew had to fill in the hole before play could continue."

Comiskey Park opened on July 1, 1910, and saw quite a bit of baseball history in the teens and twenties. In 1917–19 the park witnessed the World Series three years in a row, all of them quite memorable. In 1917 the White Sox prevailed four games to two over the New York Giants in what would be their only World Series victory in Comiskey Park. In 1918 the fall classic returned to Comiskey, but it was the Chicago Cubs who called the park home, losing to the Red Sox and the overwhelming play of a young Babe Ruth, his last year in Boston. In 1919 the Sox hosted and lost a World Series that they were accused of throwing.

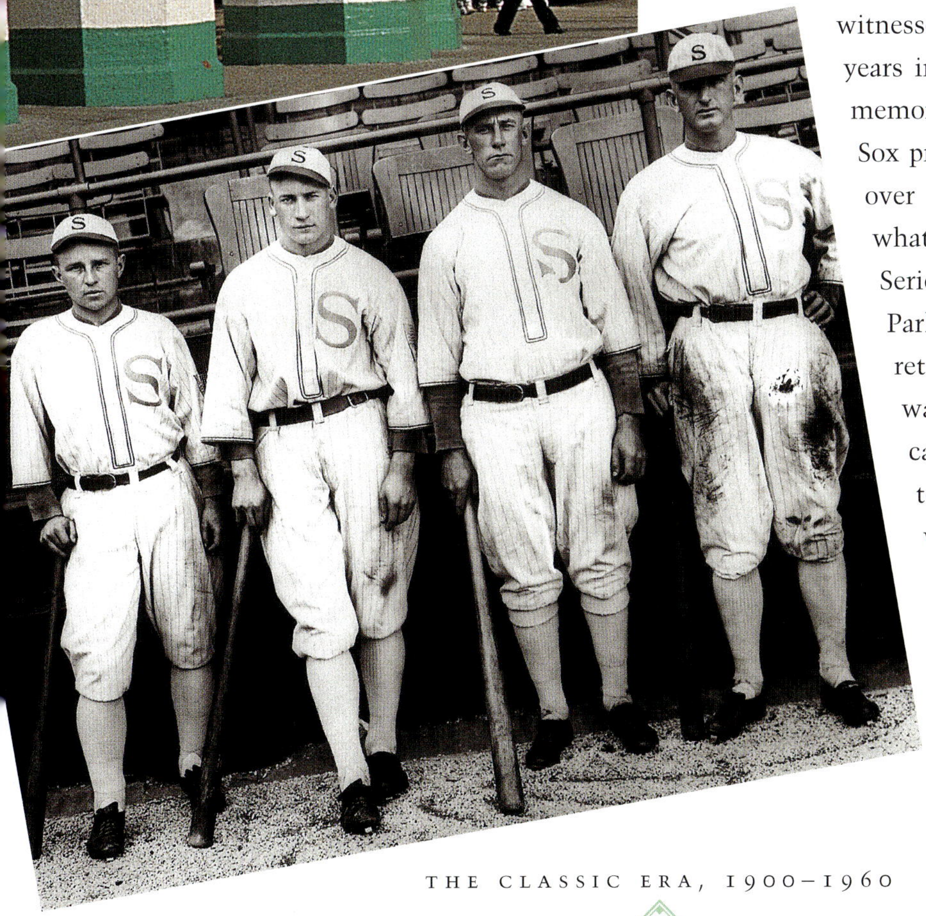

ABOVE: *The slick new Comiskey Park, which opened in 1991.* **LEFT:** *Joe Jackson (far right) and other White Sox players in 1917, two years before the infamous "Black Sox" scandal.*

ABOVE, TOP: *Baseball's first commissioner, Kennisaw Mountain Landis, throws out the first pitch at Comiskey Park on July 1, 1910.* **ABOVE, BOTTOM:** *With some seats behind metal posts, Comiskey Park represented all that was industrial about Chicago's south side.* **RIGHT:** *Vintage White Sox beer coasters.*

When it was all over, Shoeless Joe Jackson and the infamous Black Sox had created a baseball controversy that lives on to this day.

Before the 1927 season Comiskey Park was substantially remodeled. The grandstands and the bleachers were double-decked, increasing the capacity to 52,000. At the same time, center field expanded to 440 feet (134m), further cementing Comiskey's reputation as the pitcher's best friend. Comiskey Park's massive scale intimidated all but one: Babe Ruth, who slugged the only ball ever hit out of Comiskey Park, in the fall of 1927. In 1934 home plate was moved 14 feet (4m) forward to give the newly acquired Sox slugger Al Simmons an advantage in the home run department. But Simmons turned out to be a paper tiger when the home runs didn't materialize, then a real Tiger when he was shipped off to Detroit in 1936. Home plate was moved back in 1937.

The White Sox had a long history of tinkering with their ballpark to achieve home-field advantage. In the late 1940s Sox general manager Frank Lane had the habit of moving the outfield fences depending on what team was visiting, leading the league to pass the "Lane Rule" limiting fence movements to one a year. But the most memorable field dabbling came from the ground crew. In the late '60s Comiskey's field was overseen by the infamous Bossard family, who to this day remain the recognized experts in groundskeeping. Among the numerous tricks employed by the Comiskey groundskeepers were cutting the grass long or short to assist Sox fielders, and raising and lowering the mound to upset visiting pitchers' rhythm.

In March 1959 the White Sox were bought by a syndicate headed by Bill "Voom Voom" Veeck, and the fun really began. He immediately painted the park white, and installed picnic tables within view of the park. But his most outlandish renovation was the addition of baseball's first exploding scoreboard in 1960. Costing $30,000, Veeck's technological wonder stood 130 feet (40m) tall in center field and was designed to blow its top every time a White Sox player hit a home run. Nicknamed the Monster, the scoreboard unleashed a thirty-two-second cacophony of sirens, horns, and fireworks, all to the tune of the *William Tell* Overture. Fans went wild, though visiting teams were not impressed; Detroit manager Jimmy Dykes was known to have whined, "What is this, Disneyland?" But the last word on the Monster came from Casey Stengel's Yankees, who stood in front of the bullpen waving sparklers when Yankee third baseman Clete Boyer hit one over the fence in 1960.

Due to failing health, Veeck sold the club in 1961 and moved to the East Coast, but by 1975 Veeck was back in the pink. He reacquired the White Sox, and the wild promotions continued. None topped the now-infamous "Disco Demolition Night" held at Comiskey Park on July 12, 1979. Fans were encouraged to bring their disco records to the stadium, which were to be burned between games of a doubleheader against the Detroit Tigers. More than 47,000 attended, but the sight of thousands of disco records burning in center field proved too much for the fans, who rioted and stormed the field, causing the White Sox to forfeit the nightcap to the Tigers.

Veeck sold the White Sox in 1981 to a syndicate of Chicago businessmen led by Jerry Reinsdorf. The new owners looked into renovating Comiskey but ultimately deemed Comiskey too old and outdated, and threatened to move the team if a new stadium wasn't built. With communities in Florida and Wisconsin attempt-

ing to lure the White Sox with promises of fancy new stadiums, the Illinois Legislature designated funds for a new Comiskey Park to be built across the street from the old one. The last game at the old Comiskey Park was played on September 30, 1990, against the Seattle Mariners.

To this day old Comiskey Park still holds a place in the hearts of many White Sox fans. While many agree that the old park had seen better days, critics say that although the new Comiskey Park provides more amenities, it lacks the character of the old yard. Some describe the new Comiskey Park, which opened in 1991, as a cold and impersonal park whose steep upper decks serve only the interests of luxury-box revenue. But though the new White Sox yard has its critics, even the staunchest fans admit it was time for the old Comiskey to hit the showers. Chicago native and lifelong Sox fan Jeff Magid remembers visiting the old Comiskey shortly before its closing:

> Looking around Comiskey with the realization that it would be demolished, I recalled the exciting games I'd seen in my youth. I duly noted all the metal posts I sat behind. Then awash in memories as I left the stadium, my thoughts were simply this: WHAT A DUMP THIS BALLPARK IS! IT HAS ALL THE CHARM OF A STEEL MILL! GOOD RIDDANCE!

Some say the new Comiskey Park, with its ultra-steep upper deck, lacks the charm and intimacy of its predecessor.

Polo Grounds

New York (1911–63)

The home of the New York Giants for forty-six years, the Polo Grounds was a hallowed hall of baseball history. As one of the famous troika of New York ballparks that also included Yankee Stadium and Ebbets Field, the Polo Grounds was home to not one but three major league teams. Besides the Giants, both the Yankees and the Mets called the Polo Grounds home at one time or another.

Irrespective of the field's name, polo was never played at the Polo Grounds. The longtime home of the New York Giants was in fact the fourth park to carry the name. In 1883 John B. Day brought his independent team, the Metropolitans, from Brooklyn to a former polo sight near Central Park after getting a tip on the site from a shoeshine boy. Day's team played at this original Polo Grounds for five years, until they were evicted by the city of New York after the 1888 season.

For the 1889 season Day moved his team to a spot just under Coogan's Bluff, between 155th and 159th streets. In fact, there were two ball-

BELOW: *Bleachers at the Polo Grounds.* **RIGHT:** *The Polo Grounds centerfield, shown in 1954, was challenging in terms of its depth, but with both foul poles under 300 feet (91m), the park delighted pull hitters like Babe Ruth.*

LONGINES
A HIT!
REGULAR
& KING-SIZE
CHESTERFIELD

The New York Mets moved to the cavernous Shea Stadium after they spent their first two seasons (1962 and 1963) in the far more intimate Polo Grounds.

parks in Coogan's Bluff: the Giants brought the name "Polo Grounds" to the southern half, while the upstart Players League occupied the northern half of the meadow in a yard they called Brotherhood Park. The two parks were located so close to each other that home runs in one park would land in the other, causing the fans from both parks to cheer! But by the 1891 season the Players League had gone belly-up, and the National League took over the northern part of the meadow, bringing the Polo Grounds moniker with them.

This third Polo Grounds consisted of little more than a double-decked wooden grandstand, with bleachers in the outfield. The park held 16,000, including a spot in center field for well-heeled patrons to park their carriages. But this Polo Grounds was short-lived as well—the park burned to the ground on April 14, 1911. Less than three months later the Polo Grounds rose again, with temporary stands. By the time the Philadelphia Athletics rolled into town for the 1911 World Series, the Polo Grounds sported steel-and-concrete grandstands, and a capacity of more than 30,000.

The Polo Grounds inherited another tenant when the Yankees moved in for the 1913 season and stayed ten years. When the Giants met the Yankees in back-to-back World Series in 1922 and 1923, every game of the fall classic was played at the Polo Grounds. Relative harmony between the two teams existed for six years until 1919, when the Yankees acquired Babe Ruth from the Red Sox. Ruth cherished the short fences of the Polo Grounds, and his frequent home runs were making the Yankees the darlings of the box office. This success thrilled fans but irked John McGraw, the fiercely competitive owner of the Giants. The Yankees were booted from the Polo Grounds in 1922, and in 1923 took up residence in Yankee Stadium, their new palace located just across the Harlem River in the Bronx. But the exit was not without some regret on the part of Ruth, who had done so well at the Polo Grounds. "Boy, how I used to sock 'em in there," Ruth lamented. "I cried when they took me out of the Polo Grounds."

Looking at the unique dimensions of the Polo Grounds, one can understand Ruth's love for the park. The stadium was modeled in a bathtub shape, which allowed for incredibly short distances at the foul poles—279 feet (85m) in left field and 257 feet (78m) in right. And if that wasn't enough to make hitters salivate, the Polo Grounds featured a second-deck overhang in left field that extended beyond the bottom deck, making the home run distance to the upper deck a mere 258 feet (79m) in left.

Center field and the power alleys at the Polo Grounds were perilously long. From an aerial view of the park, the most obvious feature of the submarine-shaped sandlot was the endless expanse of green outfield. The center field wall was 483 feet (147m) from home plate for most of the park's life, an insurmountable distance by any standard. It has been argued that one of the most famous plays in baseball history, Willie Mays's backhanded catch of a Vic Wertz fly ball in the 1954 World Series, never could have occurred in most other parks, where such a smash would have easily been a home run.

The Giants played decades of glorious baseball in the Polo Grounds, but by the late 1950s the sport was changing. The riches of California were beckoning, and the Giants' days in the Polo Grounds were numbered. With sagging attendance, owner Horace Stoneham announced in 1957 that the team was vacating Harlem for San Francisco. "We're sorry to disappoint the kids of New York," Stoneham is quoted as saying in *Baseball: An Illustrated History*, "but we didn't see many of their parents out there at the Polo Grounds in recent years."

For Giants fans, the impossible became reality on September 29, 1957, when the Giants played their last game in the Polo Grounds, losing to the Pirates 9–1. Only 11,606 fans bothered to show up, some in center field waving a large banner that read "Stay Team, Stay."

Five years later the Polo Grounds was open for baseball again, if only temporarily. The newly minted New York Mets called the Polo Grounds home for two years while Shea Stadium was going up in Flushing, Queens. The fledgling ball club pumped $250,000 into the Polo Grounds to bring it up to speed. But after the Mets spent two years setting new records for losing (they gave up 120 games in 1962), the Polo Grounds were empty again. The old yard was demolished on April 10, 1964, devastated by the same wrecking ball that had razed Ebbets Field just a few years earlier.

ABOVE: *A program from the 1912 World Series. The Giants' stadium was originally called Brush Stadium, a name that never stuck.* **BELOW:** *A vintage postcard from the Polo Grounds.*

Tiger Stadium

Detroit (1912–99)

Baseball today is caught in a tug-of-war between the past and the present, and the game struggles to retain its glorious history while keeping up with the economic realities of the present. No major league ballpark in the United States symbolized this battle of old versus new more than Detroit's Tiger Stadium. Before the battle was over, Tiger Stadium would sit at the middle of a unique owner-fan struggle that ended up in the Michigan Supreme Court.

Located for almost nine decades at the historic corner of Michigan and Trumbull Avenues in Detroit, Tiger Stadium has one of the most colorful and controversial histories in baseball. In 1895 George Vanderbeck looked to convert a Detroit hay market into a park for his Detroit Western League team. Bennett Park, named after a Detroit player who'd lost both his legs in a train accident, was little more than a wooden grandstand holding fewer than 10,000 fans when it went up in 1896. The modest park saw a tremendous amount of baseball, including the debut of the great Ty Cobb and three straight American League pennants (which led to three straight World Series losses) from 1907 to 1909.

By 1911 the Tigers were so popular that a bigger stadium was required, and new owner Frank Navin shelled out $300,000 for a new baseball palace that would hold 23,000 fans on the same location. Opening day for the new Navin Field, as it was originally called, was delayed two days because of rain, but the new park opened on April 20, 1912 (coincidentally, the same day

ABOVE: *A pennant from the 1951 All-Star game, when the Detroit Tigers' ballpark was called Briggs Stadium.* **RIGHT:** *Historic Tiger Stadium, with its infamous right field "porch."*

Bud
Office DEPOT
1-800-FIRST USA
DTE Energy
2 5 6 16
42
TIGER HALL OF FAMERS

An overhead view of the original Tiger Stadium in Detroit. Originally opened in 1912, the ballpark closed its turnstiles for good at the end of the 1999 season.

that Fenway Park opened). Upon opening, Navin Field was little more than concrete-and-steel grandstands that extended beyond the bases, with small bleachers in right field. To the excitement—and benefit—of team owners, the new stadium required the demolition of a row of houses located behind the old left field, eliminating a series of rooftop "wildcat bleachers" that had been erected by bootleg fans.

The stadium saw a number of renovations, the first of which occurred in 1924. A second deck was added to the grandstands, which increased capacity to 30,000. In 1935, the year the Tigers took the World Series, new owner Walter Briggs looked to enlarge the stadium but, as Michael Gershman describes in *Diamonds: The Evolution of the Ballpark*, he ran into a problem expanding amidst tight urban confines. "Trumbull Avenue ran right behind it," Gershman wrote, "and there was no way to expand backward. Another problem was that Briggs didn't want to cheapen the home run by moving the wall in any way closer than 325 feet [99m]. Right field was shortened from 367 to 325 feet [112 to 99m], but to compensate, he extended the upper deck 10 feet [3m] beyond the lower deck in front and in back." The result was a "porch" hanging over the field onto which cunning hitters could bloop home runs. The home run porch became an indelible symbol of this old ball yard, and was the inspiration for a similar design at the Ballpark in Arlington, home of the Texas Rangers.

By 1938, the stadium (now called Briggs Stadium after its new owner) had undergone more expansion and reached a capacity of 58,000. Little change occurred in the new stadium in the succeeding years, except for the addition of lights in 1948 (the last American League Park to do so) and a name change to Tiger Stadium in 1961. While new ballparks habitually pulled in home run fences to increase long-ball action, Tiger Stadium's center field continued to stand at 440 feet (134m), one of the longest in the majors.

By the 1960s, with new multipurpose cathedrals popping up all over the country, Detroit remained faithful to its historic park. Writer Michael Gershman comments on Detroit's ironic pride in their ballpark, writing, "Such an attitude would be noteworthy anywhere in the United States; it is doubly so in Detroit, America's capital of planned obsolescence, a city whose civic leaders think not in generations or decades but in model years."

The fans at Tiger Stadium saw their Detroit team win three more Series, the first two in 1945 and 1968. But it was the 1984 World Series that made headlines for more than the play on the field. In the fifth and deciding game of the series, Kirk Gibson popped two out of the park to take the World Series from the San Diego Padres, and the Detroit faithful celebrated by going nuts. Fans stormed onto the field and destroyed the turf, and a riot broke out on the street. In the end, the fiasco ignited more than the cars that burned outside the stadium: the 1984 World Series riot heightened the debate over whether Tiger Stadium was ready for replacement.

Through the 1980s and 1990s Tiger owners and supporters went back and forth over whether Tiger Stadium should be bulldozed or renovated. Detractors questioned the stadium's structural integrity, as well as the safety of the surrounding neighborhood, while supporters argued that owners were more interested in profits and luxury boxes than in history. Manager Sparky Anderson, who led the team to the 1984 World Series victory, weighed in by saying, "Those who want to preserve Tiger Stadium and keep it for their grandchildren have lost their marbles." However, preservationists proved to be crazy like foxes, and well organized. In 1987 fans united against the new ballpark formed the Tiger Stadium Fan Club, a group that turned out to be a formidable adversary in the fight for the future of the old park.

The Tiger Stadium Fan Club and the team owners continued to argue over the fate of Tiger Stadium for years. In 1988, the fan club pulled a coup by getting Tiger Stadium placed on the National Register of Historic Places. This was significant because it meant that no federal funds could be used to tear down Tiger Stadium and build a replacement on the site. But the boldest move came in January 1990, as the Tiger Stadium Fan Club made the unprecedented move of releasing its own plan for the preservation of Tiger Stadium. Dubbed the Cochrane Plan, after the name of an adjoining street, the plan was a Magna Carta for ballpark preservationists.

Nevertheless, Tiger owners, along with city and state officials, continued to pursue a new stadium. Even an $8 million renovation to Tiger Stadium in 1993 (which included a new scoreboard and other amenities) didn't stop the new-stadium tidal wave. In 1995 the Tiger Stadium Fan Club initiated a lawsuit challenging the funding for a proposed new ballpark. This unprecedented fan rebellion went all the way to the Michigan Supreme Court, which ruled against the lawsuit on July 17, 1996. In the end, with a court victory and money in their pocket, Tiger owners broke ground for a new ballpark on October 27, 1997.

The Tigers' new ballpark debuted on opening day 2000 and, in a sign of the times, is called Comerica Park after the financial services company that paid millions for the naming rights. The new park is everything the rule book says it should be: with no upper-deck seats in the outfield, Comerica Park features a stunning view of the Detroit skyline. A cozy sandlot holding 42,000, the new Tiger yard has a classic brick facade and a massive entrance with two 60-foot (18m) baseball bats and a massive Tiger statue guarding the entrance.

For the city of Detroit, the end of professional baseball at Tiger Stadium was the end of a long and emotional struggle that wrote an important chapter in the history of American ballparks. As teams struggle to find new sources of revenue in order to compete for players, the faithful continue to debate the future of the game's ancient ballparks. And nowhere has this clash been more obvious than in Detroit. For better or for worse, Major League Baseball no longer calls the corner of Michigan and Trumbull home.

A newly installed seat awaits a fan during construction at Comerica Park.

Fenway Park

Boston (opened 1912)

For the Boston baseball fanatic, there is nothing like the frenzied activity in front of Fenway Park prior to a Red Sox game. Fans dash in and out of cafes while the adjoining Yawkey Way swarms with vendors. Walking the perimeter of Fenway Park, the home of the Red Sox for almost nine decades, you can't help but feel the electricity of Boston and the city's love of its ballpark.

Bostonians have been experiencing Fenway's unique baseball magic since the park opened on April 20, 1912, the same day as Detroit's Tiger Stadium. And with the demise of the Motor City ballpark after the 1999 season, Fenway now stands as the oldest major league park in commission, a standard-bearer whose beauty and history have cast a spell over purists and reformers alike.

From 1901–1911, the Boston Pilgrims—predecessors to the Red Sox—played ball at the Huntington Avenue Grounds, which today is part of Northeastern University in Boston. In 1904, *Boston Globe* owner General Charles Taylor bought the Red Sox for his son John, and the younger Taylor immediately made plans for a new ballpark to be located in a swampy part of Boston known as the fens. The area had been drained a few years earlier when Frederick Law Olmsted, who designed New York's Central Park, planned a ring of parks surrounding Boston. By the time the Red Sox were ready for their new park, the fens became an ideal location, mainly because the senior Taylor was a substantial shareholder in the Fenway Realty Company, which owned the land.

Together with Forbes Field in Pittsburgh and Shibe Park in Philadelphia (both of which opened in 1909), Fenway was one of a new generation of concrete-and-steel ballparks. Opening day saw Boston mayor John "Honey Fitz" Fitzgerald (grandfather of John F. Kennedy) throw out the first pitch at a ballpark that was quite different from the Fenway Park we know today. The original Fenway had a massive center field measuring 488 feet (149m)—almost 50 feet (15m) longer than it is now. Wooden bleachers and grandstands sat in the outfield. But the real story was in left field. Long before Fenway had a massive green wall as its trademark, left field was known for the 10-foot (3m) embankment that led up to the fence. So treacherous was this

BELOW: *Red Sox great Ted Williams featured on a label for Moxie, a popular soft drink in 1950s Boston.*

RIGHT: *The Philadelphia Athletics warm up in Fenway Park.* **OPPOSITE:** *Before it acquired its infamous color in 1947, Fenway's "Green Monster" was covered with a rainbow of advertisements.*

CITIES SERVICE
PM
Pleasant Moments
"O.K. IF YOU AVOID 5 O'CLOCK SHADOW."
GEM
BLADES
The RED SOX
use...
LIFEBUOY
HEALTH SOAP
AMERICAN LEAGUE
FENWAY PARK
AMERICAN LEAGUE
NATIONAL LEAGUE

ABOVE: *Towering 37 feet (11.3m) high, Fenway Park's Green Monster has been taunting hitters for more than fifty years.* **RIGHT:** *The Red Sox pitching staff, including a young Babe Ruth (second from right), right before the Bambino was traded to the Yankees.*

incline that it became known as Duffy's Cliff in honor of Red Sox left fielder Duffy Lewis, one of the few players who mastered the slope.

Shallow-pocketed owners prevented any major renovations to Fenway for the next two decades; even after a fire on May 8, 1926, owner Bob Quinn did nothing more than haul off the burnt remains of the left-field bleachers. But Fenway received a large cash infusion before the 1934 season, when new owner Tom Yawkey bought the team. Duffy's Cliff was leveled, and wooden bleachers were replaced with concrete grandstands in right field. The most enduring improvement made in 1934 was the addition of a 37-foot (11.3m) fence erected in left field, a Fenway landmark that remains to this day. Constructed of 18 feet (5.5m) of concrete topped by 19 feet (5.8m) of wooden railroad ties covered with tin, the wall that would someday become known as the Monster was originally littered with advertising.

A ladder was attached in 1936 so that batting practice home runs could be shagged, and to this day remains the only "in play" ladder in the majors. Starting at just over 13 feet (4m) and going to the top of the wall, the Fenway ladder is considered a charming feature by most, except Sox great Ted Williams, who once watched a fly ball hit by Jim Lemon careen off the ladder and into center field for an in-the-park home run.

In 1947 Fenway underwent another renovation and the wall got its infamous coat of green paint, becoming the Green Monster we know today. This great wall of baseball has challenged a series of Red Sox fielders, from Ted Williams to Carl Yastrzemski. By 1975 the tin of the Green Monster had seen better days, and the wall was replaced with a hard plastic surface.

Nothing is more identified with Fenway Park than that intimidating, towering left-field fence. Loved by pitchers, feared by hitters, and revered by baseball writers, the Green Monster is one of the most endearing (and enduring) symbols of ballpark uniqueness. While many parks have built tall outfield fences, none has the mystique and allure of Fenway's Green Monster.

To this day, Fenway Park (along with Wrigley Field) stands as one of the grand old parks of the game. But unfortunately, with its outdated facilities and cramped seating, Fenway may not be long for this world. Like the struggle that raged over the fate of Detroit's Tiger Stadium, Red Sox owners and fans have argued for years about whether to renovate Fenway Park or bulldoze it. While there are those who complain that without the additional revenue from luxury boxes and added amenities, it will be increasingly difficult to field a winning team, others claim Fenway is their own, a civic treasure to be preserved at all costs. It's a familiar battle, but one with a twist.

In a brilliant move, Red Sox officials released plans in 1999 for a new $545 million park that is an updated replica of Fenway Park, with all the modern amenities added. The proposed new Fenway Park, which would open in 2003, would be located across the street from the current stadium. It would even feature the existing Green Monster in left field. So similar are the old and new parks that *Baseball Weekly* columnist Paul White reported that the blueprints for the two parks are virtually indistinguishable. "I laid the two plans side-by-side in front of some folks who have more than a soft spot for the existing park," White wrote in a May 1999 column. "They weren't sure which version was the renovation, thought [*sic*] either could be."

Best intentions aside, proponents of a new park can be sure to get a fight from Save Fenway Park, a grassroots organization designed to preserve the old sandlot. But in the end, the smart money has the Red Sox vacating Fenway, leaving Wrigley Field as the sole remaining major league park built in the first two decades of the twentieth century.

ABOVE: *A vintage Red Sox pennant.* **BELOW:** *Carl Yastrzemski was inducted into the Hall of Fame in 1989 after spending his entire twenty-three-year career with the Boston Red Sox.*

BUILD THE HOUSE THAT MERCY NEEDS... SUPPORT BROOKLYN RED CROSS BUILDING FUND
SHINE
FFIN
UR SHOES
MICHAELS-CO.
6 BIG Furniture STORES
THE BRASS RAIL
FULTON AT NEVINS · BROOKLYN
Schaefer
Be Happy
GO LUCKY!
LUCKY STRIKE
351 FT.
BUY TYDOL
GASOLINE
Natural Gas is Here!
THE BROOKLYN UNION GAS COMPANY
Manufacturers Trust Company
FLORSHEIM SHOES
STADLERS
42

Ebbets Field

Brooklyn (1913–57)

Built on the site of a garbage yard known as Pigtown, Ebbets Field turned a dump into a palace of baseball, and after its demise, into an urban legend. "Of all the ballparks that no longer exist," wrote Lawrence Ritter in his classic book *Lost Ballparks,* "none have been romanticized more than Ebbets Field."

The lost Mecca of ballparks, Ebbets Field had physical characteristics so recognizable that they've become stereotypes. The small dimensions of Ebbets Field enabled fans to be so close to the game they were, in the words of announcer Red Barber, "practically an infielder." The park's home run fences were peppered with advertisements, including clothier Abe Stark's legendary billboard that read, "Hit sign, win suit." And if you're looking for the inspiration for the brick facades of San Francisco's Pacific Bell Park or Baltimore's Camden Yards, look no further than Ebbets Field, whose magnificent brick entrance tempted the faithful into an Italian marble rotunda. The floor tiles represented the stitches on a baseball, and from the 27-foot (8m) ceiling hung a chandelier with twelve baseball-bat arms, each holding baseball-shaped globes.

Longing to move out of Washington Park, a cramped firetrap that the Dodgers called home, owner Charles Ebbet built the new jewel in 1913. Ebbet believed the baseball fan should be "taken care of" and sunk $750,000, an obscene amount of money for the day, into his new edifice. But before it was done, Ebbet had to sell half his interest in the team to pay for it.

The original park consisted of double-decked grandstands extending 30 feet (9m) past the infield, and holding

LEFT: *Duke Snider belts one over the Ebbets Field scoreboard during the first game of the 1952 World Series.*

BELOW: *A Dodger yearbook from 1954, depicting the team's dream of a new stadium. Three years later they got their wish with a move to Los Angeles.*

BELOW: *Dodger Duke Snider lunges for a ball against the fence at Ebbets Field in 1954.* **RIGHT:** *The Brooklyn faithful cheer for their beloved "Bums."* **OPPOSITE:** *Future Hall of Famer Jackie Robinson walks home from Ebbets Field on April 16, 1947, just one day after he broke the color barrier.*

just 25,000 people. After the the 1931 season the grandstands were expanded to increase capacity to 32,000. The right-field wall and scoreboard was said to have more than 289 different angles, and playing the outfield at Ebbets was reputed to be so tricky that tips were passed on through generations of Dodger fielders.

Ebbets Field was initially a pitcher's park. Upon completion in 1913, center field was a distant 450 feet (137m), and ballooned to an unachievable 466 feet (142m) in 1930. The only manageable fence was right field, at 301 feet (92m). Gradually over the years, though, as more outfield seating was added, the home run distances were reduced to mortal dimensions, and by the 1940s the center field had come in 50 feet (15m). Right field was topped by a 38-foot (11.5m) fence, and balls hitting the fence were considered to be in play.

The Dodgers prospered in their years at Ebbets Field, winning the pennant nine times and the World Series once. But on April 15, 1947, Ebbets Field gave fans one of the greatest thrills in the history of the game, when Jackie Robinson took the field for the Dodgers, breaking the game's infamous color barrier, and marking the beginning of the end of baseball's deepest travesty.

Brooklynites loved their ballpark and their team, whom they affectionately called "Dem Bums." But in the end, even though Dodger owner Walter O'Malley was making good money, the Dodgers' future in Brooklyn looked dim. The Dodgers "were one of the richest teams in baseball," write Geoffrey Ward and Ken Burns in *Baseball: An Illustrated History*, "but despite the brilliant baseball played . . . the crowds that came out to see them were smaller with each passing season."

O'Malley laid it on the line for New York: he wanted a new ballpark or he was pulling up stakes for the baseball-hungry West Coast. It was an ironic ultimatum both for its historic precedent (Charles Ebbet had originally bought the team in 1902 to prevent a move to Baltimore) and for the way it foreshadowed the ballpark-relocation games so common today. Unable to gain a new ball yard, and with the riches of Los Angeles beckoning, O'Malley looked to go west. In 1957 the National League owners voted to allow him to do just that.

The Dodgers played their last game at Ebbets Field on September 24, 1957, and only 6,702 people bothered to show up. A few years later, on February 23, 1960, Lucy Monroe sang the national anthem at Ebbets Field, just as she had many times before. Moments later, a two-ton wrecking ball brought down Ebbets Field and broke the heart of Brooklyn.

EBBETS

ABOVE: *Even without a recent World Series, there's plenty of baseball history on Chicago's north side: Sammy Sosa slams his sixty-second home run of the year at Wrigley Field on September 13, 1998.*

Wrigley Field

Chicago (opened 1914)

To most baseball fans, ballparks begin and end with Wrigley Field. From its ivy-covered walls to its timeless manually operated scoreboard, Wrigley Field is the standard against which today's new "retro" ballparks are judged. The home of the Chicago Cubs is the second oldest ballpark in the majors, preceded only by Boston's Fenway Park (built in 1912).

Wrigley was built in 1914 by restaurant magnate Charlie Weeghman, who housed his Federal League Chicago Whales there until the upstart league went belly-up in 1915. Weeghman put together an investor group, bought the Chicago Cubs from the Taft family of Cincinnati, and moved the team to his two-year-old ballpark on the corner of Clark and Addison on Chicago's north side. The Cubs played their first game at the park in April 1916.

Weeghman Park, as Wrigley was then known, was a modest little park, holding only 14,000 and costing a mere $250,000 to build. By 1920 chewing-gum king William Wrigley, Jr., had bought out Weeghman and changed the name to Cubs Park, and in 1926 to Wrigley Field. That same year the grandstands were doubled and the capacity blossomed to more than 38,000.

In 1937 the outfield grandstands were erected and a new, bright-green scoreboard went up, ordered by Bill Veeck, who would later invent the exploding scoreboard across town at Comiskey Park. Operated by a team of ladder-climbing number-posters, this new technical marvel featured in-progress scores and pitcher's numbers. The numbers indicating batter, ball, strike, and out, along with "H" and "E" to signify hit and miss, were shaped like eyes. A mechanical clock was added to the top of the scoreboard in 1941. Traditional yet imposing, the 25- by 75-foot (7.6x23m) Wrigley Field scoreboard is considered the standard by which all other scoreboards are judged. It has passed the test of time, and lumber. To this day, no batter has hit it, although Roberto Clemente and Bill Nicholson have come close.

Outfield bleachers were added in 1937 and Veeck, inspired by the ivy walls he had seen at a stadium in Indianapolis, ordered trees and plants in center field. In all, 350 Japanese bittersweet plants and 200 Boston ivy plants were planted, as well as 8 Chinese elm trees in pots on the bleacher steps. But the fierce Lake Michigan wind soon made twigs of the trees, and the bittersweet plants bit the dust as well. The ivy survived, however, and continues to cover the outfield walls to this day. In fact, the house rules at Wrigley Field even provide for the ivy, as any ball that gets stuck in the vines is a ground-rule double.

Wrigley is a field of firsts. In 1941 the Cubs became the first major league team to serenade their fans with organ music. Wrigley was the first park where fans could keep balls hit for home runs, but it is also where fans started throwing back opponent's home run balls. And when fans complained of vendors blocking their view, Wrigley was the first park to construct permanent concession stands.

This Chicago landmark has seen its share of historic events, but none more so than Babe Ruth's historic "called shot" in the 1932 World Series. Although it has long been debated whether Ruth actually telegraphed his dinger, there's no doubt that Ruth gave a gesture to center field right before slamming one out. Intentional or not, journalists had a field day, one saying Ruth "pointed to the spot where he expected to send his rapier home." Many years later, even Ruth himself questioned whether he actually called the shot, but the resulting homer is one of the many historic legacies of Wrigley Field.

Wrigley Field has changed delightfully little since its early days. In fact, Wrigley was the last ballpark in the majors to install lights—it was day games only until 1988, when Major League Baseball threatened to make the Cubs play post-

season ball in St. Louis unless lights were installed. But even that bit of modernization has done little to diminish the charm of Wrigley.

Chicago ferociously loves the Cubs and their crown jewel of a ballpark. On any game day the city streets surrounding the park can look more like Mardi Gras than Chicago's north side. Maybe it's just blind optimism, since the Cubs have never won a World Series in Wrigley (their last was 1908, six years before Wrigley was built). As longtime fan and Chicago native Doug McConnell tells it, "Walk onto Addison Street after a Friday-night Cub victory, with mobs of people and bands playing in the street, and you'd think they'd won the World Series!"

TOP: *Ticket to the 1947 All-Star game held at Wrigley Field.* **CENTER:** *Wrigley's trademark ivy-covered outfield walls are among the park's most distinctive characteristics.* **BOTTOM:** *Wrigley Field remains very much the same as it was when it opened in 1914, to the delight of baseball fans of all stripes.*

YANKEE STADIUM
MAIN ENTRANCE
GRAND STAND
GRAND STAND

Yankee Stadium

New York (opened 1923)

Some ballparks are beautiful buildings, architectural monuments whose palatial surroundings inspire and awe. Other ballparks stand out for the historic games and fantastic athletes they have showcased. For the combination of heavenly events and hallowed halls, no other ball yard holds a candle to Yankee Stadium. Peering onto the field from the grandstand gives one an overwhelming feeling, an immense appreciation of both the stadium itself and the players it has seen.

The Yankee dynasty at East 161st Street and River Avenue in the Bronx actually started before a single shovel of dirt was turned over. In fact, the origins of pinstripe domination date back to 1919, when the Yankees acquired Babe Ruth from the Red Sox. At that time the Yankees shared the Polo Grounds with the Giants, an arrangement in effect since 1913. But with the slugging Ruth in tow, the Yankees were not only starting to dominate the standings, they were pulling in the crowds as well. The Polo Grounds' slugger-friendly home run fences left home run territory wide open, and Ruth's frequent homers were soon stealing the show in New York.

And so out Ruth went, along with the rest of the team, with an eviction notice served by the Giants in 1921 (the Yanks vacated after the 1922 season). So intense was their rivalry that Giants owners were willing to do just about anything in their quest for victory, even trying to force the Yankees out of business. "If we kick them out they won't be able to find another location on Manhattan Island," the Giants' John McGraw said at the time. "The fans will forget about them and they will be through."

But banishment to the Bronx, on the other side of the Harlem River, was far from a fatal blow for the Yankees, who finished their massive new ballpark in time for the 1923 season. To the contrary, it gave them an edifice in proportion to their growing

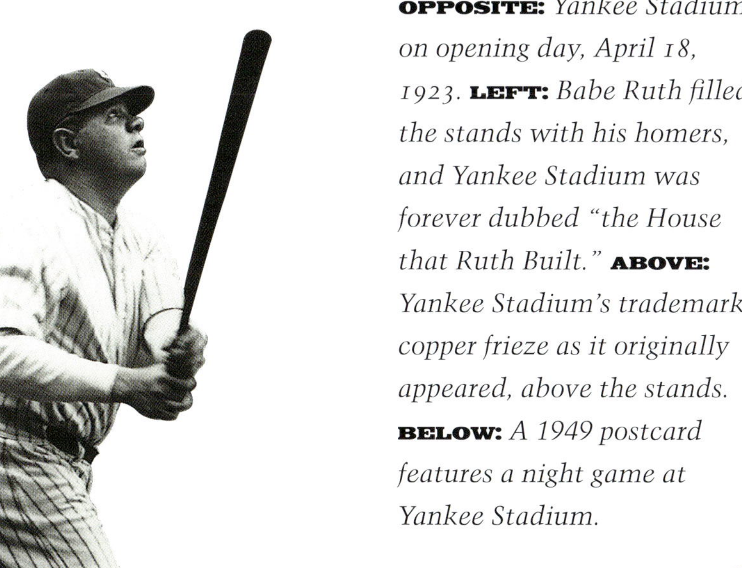

OPPOSITE: *Yankee Stadium on opening day, April 18, 1923.* **LEFT:** *Babe Ruth filled the stands with his homers, and Yankee Stadium was forever dubbed "the House that Ruth Built."* **ABOVE:** *Yankee Stadium's trademark copper frieze as it originally appeared, above the stands.* **BELOW:** *A 1949 postcard features a night game at Yankee Stadium.*

ABOVE: *Program from the 1941 World Series.* **BELOW:** *All of Yankee Stadium pays tribute to Babe Ruth during a ceremony to retire his uniform number in June 1948. This was to be the last time the Babe would wear Yankee pinstripes, as he passed away two months later.*

legacy. The first ballpark to be called a "stadium," Yankee Stadium was a triple-deck marvel that held 58,000 fans. The top deck was adorned with a distinctive copper frieze, which became an icon of Yankee Stadium.

From day one, Yankee Stadium was an enormous success. Opening day on April 18, 1923, saw John Philip Sousa lead a military band, and Babe Ruth hit the first home run. An *Evening Telegram* writer was so convinced of Ruth's history-making potential in his new home, he dubbed the stadium "the House that Ruth Built" and the name stuck.

Like most ballparks of its era, the original Yankee Stadium had outfield dimensions that were massive, and sometimes bizarre. Left-center field was 500 feet (152m) from home plate and deemed "Death Valley" by those unfortunate hitters trying to slug into it. In 1923 the right-field foul line and bleachers met at such an acute angle it was dubbed the "Blood Angle" for the pain right fielders experienced trying to track down a ball hit there. In case that wasn't tricky enough for batters, center field featured a flag pole in fair territory.

In 1932 a stone monument to the great Yankee manager Miller Huggins was erected in center field, followed by monuments to Lou Gehrig in 1941 and Babe Ruth in 1949. Located in fair territory, these monuments complicated plays, and sometimes even made frustrated managers evoke Yankee ghosts. Yankee manager Casey Stengel once watched with frustration as his center fielder lost a ball among the monuments, and yelled, "Ruth, Gehrig, Huggins, someone throw that darned ball in here *now!*"

The next decades saw many minor alterations to Yankee Stadium, and many more monumental baseball moments. During the 1920s and 1930s, second and third decks were added in the outfield, and wooden bleachers were replaced with concrete. As a result, center field was pulled in over 30 feet (9m) in 1937, and additional scoreboards appeared in the '40s.

While the park evolved, the games it witnessed made history. Yankee Stadium saw a home run record set by Babe Ruth in 1927, and again by Roger Maris in 1961. Don Larsen pitched a perfect World Series game there in 1956, and Yankee Stadium saw the farewell of a succession of great champions, including Ruth, Lou Gehrig, Joe DiMaggio, and Mickey Mantle.

By the 1970s time had caught up with the old ballpark, and Yankee owners contemplated becoming the New Jersey Yankees. So, while the Yankees took up residence in Shea Stadium, the ballpark underwent a major renovation in 1974 and 1975. The monuments were moved behind left-center field, and gone was the charming practice of allowing fans to exit the stadium through center field. The distinctive copper frieze that had lined the stadium was moved to a portion of center field. Armed with a new stadium, the Yankees ended the 1970s on a tear, with a dominating team that included Reggie "Mr. October" Jackson, who hit three home runs on three pitches during the 1977 World Series.

Some things never change. The last decade of the twentieth century again found the Yankees with a dominant team and uncertainty about their ballpark. Owner George Steinbrenner has raised the prospect of moving the team to New Jersey, and again the health of Yankee Stadium is questioned. Of course, it didn't help matters when, on April 13, 1998, a 500-pound (227kg) steel joint fell from the upper deck onto the seats below. Thankfully the stadium was empty so no injuries occurred, though it raised the painful thought of New York without the Yankees. The team's current lease with Yankee Stadium expires in 2002, and with terms like "multipurpose domed stadium" and "New Jersey" being tossed around, it's safe to say that the next few years could be uncertain ones for the House that Ruth Built.

ABOVE: *Yankee Stadium after the renovation of 1974–75. Notice the copper frieze was moved to the outfield.*

LEFT: *The retired numbers of Yankee greats line the walls of Yankee Stadium's Memorial Park.*

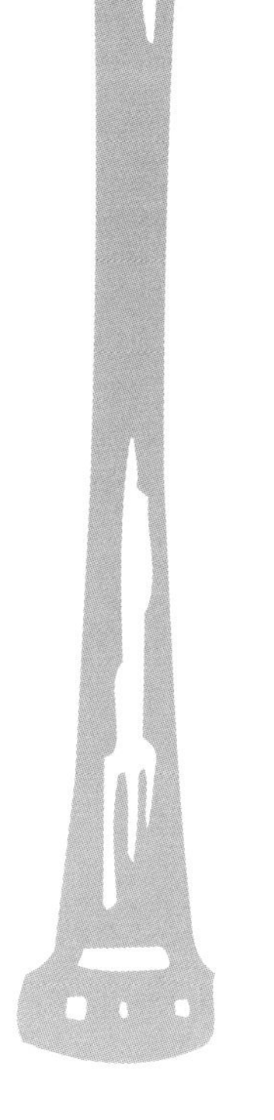

CHAPTER 2

The Modern Era, 1960–1990

By 1960 many of America's major league ballparks were considerably out of step with the times. Unfortunately, the predictable rhythm of organ music on a sunny afternoon in a small urban park was simply not meeting the modern needs of postwar society. Newly affluent mobile families looked to pack the kids into their cars and head to the ballgame. This meant two things: more seats and more parking, which dictated larger parks located outside congested city centers. It also meant that games were played at night, something for which many classic ballparks were not prepared. Profit-hungry owners looked to appease the masses, forgoing tradition in the interest of progress. By the time the Dodgers

OPPOSITE: *Toronto's ultramodern SkyDome, standing in the shadows of the massive CN Tower.*

ABOVE: *Pro Player Stadium in Miami, home of the Florida Marlins.* **OPPOSITE:** *It's not just for baseball any more: the all-weather Toronto SkyDome is billed as "The World's Greatest Entertainment Centre."*

and the Giants headed west in search of new stadiums, the pattern was clear: baseball was changing forever.

The modern era saw the lowly baseball park morph into a modern giant (many would say nightmare). Capacities often boomed up to 60,000—too great a number to enable anyone to appreciate the nuances of the game. Architectural character took a back seat to perceived functionality, as the new ballpark became a strictly utilitarian object. Gone were the cherished brick facades of the urban jewels. Towering ovals of concrete now dominated baseball's landscape. Artificial turf, first used as a Band-Aid solution when the Astrodome's roof kept out the sun and killed the natural grass, became both a groundskeeping practicality and a slap in the face of tradition.

As for permanence, the numbers speak for themselves. From 1960 to 1990, eighteen new major league ballparks went up in America, starting with Candlestick Park in 1960. By the end of the century, almost 30 percent of these yards were replaced. And of the remaining parks, only a few, such as Dodger Stadium, look as though they might withstand the test of time.

It would be too easy to look back at the ballparks of the 1960s and 1970s and dismiss them as poorly planned mistakes, although many of them were. More significantly, the era was an incredible learning period for today's ballpark architect. As the old cliché goes, you don't know what you've got until it's gone. The modern era saw the death of Ebbets Field and the Polo Grounds, both urban legends. But it also saw the demise of such lesser-known gems as Forbes Field in Pittsburgh and Crosley Field in Cincinnati, both replaced by larger-than-life stadiums. These parks can never be brought back, and we can only hope that when new sandlots go up in the future, there will be a liberal application of lessons learned.

Fiesta Sol
LOTTERY
KEN WILLIAMS
SHOPPERS DRUG MART
TIGERS
BLUE JAYS
2:55
375
400

3Com Park (formerly Candlestick Park)

San Francisco (1960–99)

Candlestick Park, renamed 3Com Park in 1995 after the computer company that bought the naming rights, is universally identified by one singular, defining characteristic. No, it's not Willie Mays's 3,000th hit, which he got at Candlestick on July 18, 1971, nor the back-to-back no-hitters thrown by the Giants' Gaylord Perry and the Cardinals' Ray Washburn on September 17 and 18, 1968. It isn't even the massive earthquake that shook the 62,000 fans who were watching the Giants play their Bay Area neighbors, the Oakland A's, in the World Series on October 17, 1989. More than anything else, Candlestick will always be remembered for one thing: atrocious weather.

Located in one of the coldest, foggiest parts of San Francisco, Candlestick became legendary for the ferocious winds that swirl around this concrete park, causing dust storms in the infield, turning home runs into pop flies, and making peanut wrappers hover in midair. One of the more enduring legends of Candlestick has Giants pitcher Stu Miller being blown off the mound during the 1961 All-Star game. (Miller later denied being tossed, saying the wind "just threw me off a little.") Dubbed "Candle-fridge" by some locals, night games are so cold that fans surviving extra-inning night games have been awarded a special "Croix de Candlestick" pin.

As a part of baseball's California gold rush of the 1950s, New York Giants owner Horace Stoneham decided to move his Giants to San Francisco after the city agreed to build him a 40,000-seat stadium with 12,000 parking spots. A plot of land on the outskirts of the city, called Candlestick Point for the jagged rocks and trees that covered it, was deemed appropriate after a splendid midmorning tour of the site by Stoneham and the mayor of San Francisco. Of course, the notorious Candlestick wind never cropped up till afternoon, so the supposedly placid site was chosen.

Almost immediately the problems began. Architect John Bolles was chosen, even though he had never designed a ballpark. The original plans called for heating pipes to run under half of the seats, but when the builders installed them five inches (12.7cm) into the concrete rather than one inch (2.54cm), the system became useless. (In 1962, maverick San Francisco lawyer Melvin Belli sued the city for the cost of his season tickets, claiming he had paid for seats that were supposed to be toasty warm, and won.)

But even grand jury investigations into the project didn't stop Candlestick from rising, and

OPPOSITE: *Candlestick Park, before a 1971 renovation enclosed the upper deck into an oval.* **BELOW:** *Willie Mays, who some say got robbed of the home run crown by the winds of Candlestick Park.*

ABOVE: *A pre-1971 Giants pennant depicting an open-outfield Candlestick Park.*
RIGHT: *An empty upper deck was a common occurrence at San Francisco's windy stadium.*

Universally hated by baseball fans and players, San Francisco's frigid stadium is now, appropriately, football-only.

on April 12, 1960, the park opened. Foreshadowing a brand of foot-in-mouth tactics that would later bring his term to a premature end, President Richard Nixon dedicated Candlestick, calling it "one of the most beautiful ballparks of all time."

Originally a concrete horseshoe, Candlestick suffered badly from the winds, which not only froze the faithful in the stands but hampered play on the field. It has been said that if Willie Mays (who hit 660 career homers) hadn't spent so many seasons at Candlestick, he and not Hank Aaron might be the all-time home run king.

With the new San Francisco 49ers looking to share the yard, the stadium was enclosed into a concrete oval in 1971. But the new design only served to create a wind tunnel in the stadium, and a massive challenge in fielding the ball. After trying to catch pop flies at Candlestick, Dodger shortstop Dave Anderson said, "You look like one of those guys in the circus balancing poles." The new design also increased the seating capacity to an astonishing 62,000, with upper-level seating seemingly miles from home plate. Artificial turf was installed the same year, and most of the resemblance to a traditional ballpark had vanished.

One of the best Candlestick horror stories comes from player-turned-manager Phil Garner: "I remember one day when I was playing third base for the Pirates and I called for a pop fly between the bag and the mound," Garner told the *Milwaukee Journal Sentinel* in 1999. "I'm coming in toward the mound to catch the ball and Willie Stargell ends up catching it in foul territory on the other side of first base!"

Candlestick saw few improvements over the years, the most noticeable being the reintroduction of a natural grass field in 1979. All the while, a succession of Giants owners struggled over what to do with their dismay on the bay. Numerous public referendums were put before San Francisco voters, who consistently voted down the use of public money in the construction of a new Giants ballpark. But in March 1996, San Francisco finally gave its approval for the construction of a new Giants ballpark, one that would be built without the use of public money for construction. With this vote, Pacific Bell Park ushered in a new economic era for ballparks, one which had the people who came to the game, and not the general public, foot the bill.

Pacific Bell Park opened in spring 2000, the first privately funded ballpark built for Major League Baseball since Dodger Stadium first swung upen its gates in 1962. In the meantime, Candlestick—now 3Com—endures, filling the need for which it wasn't designed, and yet is somehow perfectly suited: as a home for football.

Dodger Stadium

Los Angeles (opened 1962)

Popping up at the advent of the modern ballpark era, Dodger stadium is a true anomaly. In an era when large, impersonal stadiums ruled, and when sharing a stadium with football was a universal truth, Dodger Stadium emerged as one of the most perfect baseball environments ever constructed. More surprising, it continues to shine even today, since very little has changed with this pristine masterpiece in the past three and a half decades.

Rewind to 1957. The Dodgers have just announced their heartbreaking departure from Brooklyn and are perusing Los Angeles in search of a location for their new ballpark. After a helicopter ride over the city, Dodger owner Walter O'Malley fancied a 315-acre (126ha) area called Chavez Ravine, conveniently located between Pasadena and downtown Los Angeles. Close to freeways and with enough room for acres of parking, Chavez Ravine was perfect for O'Malley's modern ballpark.

Even though the land had been previously earmarked for public use, trouble started almost immediately as residents of the area called foul and refused to move. Things got ugly as squatters dug in their heels. By the spring of 1959 the sheriff came in to forcibly evict stubborn residents, who had set up a tent city. But in the end O'Malley was able to buy out most of the last remaining holdouts in Chavez Ravine to make room for his new ballpark. Later that year the site was cleared, and construction started on what would be the first privately financed ballpark since Yankee Stadium went up in 1923.

Dodger Stadium debuted on April 10, 1962, and the bar for ballpark excellence was raised considerably. With parking for 16,000 automobiles spread out on twenty-one terraced lots, Dodger Stadium was seen as a modern marvel. The new park boasted more than 3,400 trees among its 300 acres (120ha) of landscaping, with breathtaking views of the San Gabriel Mountains and the emerging downtown skyline. A far cry from the gritty urban scenes of East Coast ballparks, Dodger Stadium boldly flaunted a new brand of California baseball. To this day Dodger Stadium is meticulously manicured, and is still one of the most pristine ballparks in the major leagues.

Inside, one cannot imagine a better setting for baseball. Although it holds 56,000 fans, Dodger Stadium is deceptively intimate, with perfect sight lines and logical proportions. Every inch is designed with the fan in mind, right down to the open concourse, where fans can watch the game while waiting in line for food. Even the stadium's symmetrical dimensions, while not "retro" in feel, give the park a sense of order that seems surprisingly appropriate.

From the beginning Dodger Stadium brought success to the box office, and to the field. Since moving into their new palace, the Dodgers have hosted eight World Series and won four, beginning with a 1963 victory just one year after the yard opened. And in the attendance department, the Dodgers are consistently at the top of the standings. In 1978 Dodger Stadium was the first ballpark to host more than three million fans in a season, and has done so twelve times since.

BELOW: *Dodger players warm up in the sunshine of Dodger Stadium.*
OPPOSITE: *In the age of ugly suburban ballparks, pristine Dodger Stadium somehow got it right.*

76
Dodgers

ABOVE: *Many ballparks claim it, this one delivers—there's not a bad seat in Dodger Stadium.* **RIGHT:** *Dodger Ron Cey battles the Yankees in the 1978 World Series at Dodger Stadium.*

No game at Dodger Stadium was complete without manager Tommy Lasorda chewing out an umpire.

Not a group to mess with perfection, the Dodger organization has made few changes to the stadium since its construction. The original plans for the park called for a huge fountain in center field, and the structure was designed so that the upper decks could wrap around into the familiar "doughnut" shape, bringing the capacity to a staggering 85,000 seats. But in the end, the Dodger organizational culture prevailed, and like most other aspects of the team up to 1998, the stadium wasn't touched. Kudos to the Dodgers: Dodger Stadium is the only pre-1990 ballpark that has never changed its capacity.

Many exciting things have happened at Dodger Stadium over the years, but change was never one of them. In the last four decades of the twentieth century, the Dodger organization and their untarnished park became famous for perennial stability and success. It is ironic that the O'Malley family, the owners who were despised for taking the Dodgers out of Brooklyn, created a franchise in Los Angeles that became the standard-bearer for baseball tradition.

In 1998 the O'Malley family shocked the baseball world by selling the Los Angeles Dodgers to Rupert Murdoch's Fox Group, stating that the era of family ownership in baseball was over. Almost immediately, the new owners started tinkering with their ballpark time capsule. In the 1999 off-season, luxury suites were added to Dodger Stadium, and the dugout boxes were expanded, all in an effort to bring in more revenue. Beyond this, only time will tell if the Dodgers' new corporate owners will have the same reverence for the past that the O'Malley family had, and what effect that might have on Dodger Stadium.

The Houston Astrodome, whose light-blocking dome led to the creation of Astroturf.

Astrodome

Houston (1965–99)

With a fully enclosed dome measuring eighteen stories high, an artificial playing surface, and central air-conditioning pumping out 2.5 million cubic feet of air per minute, the Astrodome personified the era of big, multipurpose stadiums. While the rest of the baseball world also envisioned ballparks that were "multipurpose," it took the Texans to outdo everybody. Love it or hate it, there's no denying that the Astrodome was the most ostentatious flip ever to baseball tradition.

Astro owner Judge Roy Hofheinz (previously Lyndon Johnson's campaign manager) had been bitten by the geodesic dome bug of the '60s while trying to build a domed shopping mall. But after his Houston Colt .45s were awarded a National League expansion franchise, Hofheinz set his sites on the most outlandish park in the majors. By the time he was finished, the Astrodome included padded seats, futuristic "Sky Boxes," and an exploding scoreboard.

Hofheinz called his concrete marvel the "Eighth Wonder of the World" but after the first exhibition game, with the Yankees in April 1965, players were more likely to exclaim, "I wonder where the ball is!" It turned out that the translucent cream-colored panels of the dome were great for letting light into the stadium, but murder when it came to seeing fly balls. The Astro owner had a big problem on his hands, and went to great lengths to solve it. "When outfielders insisted they couldn't see the ball and several players called the conditions dangerous, Hofheinz handed out orange sunglasses," wrote author Michael Gershman in *Diamonds: The Evolution of the Ballparks*. "In self-defense, the outfielders began wearing batting helmets during games. The Astros tried ten dozen balls dyed several colors—yellow, orange, red and cerise—to no avail."

The ultimate solution solved one problem, caused another, and changed the course of ballparks for thirty years. To alleviate the glare, the roof panels were painted. But the lack of natural light made the grass die, so they tried painting the grass green. You can guess how that turned out. Finally, the Monsanto company was commissioned to come up with an artificial surface, and Astroturf was born. Controversial from the beginning, artificial turf would soon become common among new ballparks. And while owners loved the economics of the reduced groundskeeping, the new plastic grass had few advocates among baseball players. "If horses won't eat it," infielder Dick Allen once said, "I won't play on it."

For the next thirty-five years, no event was too big for the Astrodome. Evel Knievel used it to perform a world-record motorcycle jump, Billie Jean King beat Bobby Riggs there, and Elvis Presley performed his final concert at the Astrodome. But eventually time caught up to the Astros' fancy home. Even after a $60 million expansion in 1989, the star-studded dome lost its glitter, and Astro owner Drayton McLane, Jr., threatened to take his team to Virginia unless he got a new park. Hence 1999 was the final season for baseball in the Astrodome, which was to be replaced by Enron Field, a spanking new stadium with a retractable roof. As reporter John Williams noted in the *Houston Chronicle*, "Goodbye, dome sweet dome; hello poptop."

HOUSTON ASTROS

ABOVE: *No sun and artificial turf: the Astrodome shocked the baseball world when it opened in 1965.*

PAGES 66–67: *When it opened, the Astrodome was billed as "The Eighth Wonder of the World."*

Brian
McRae
Sixth in NL
with 33
stolen bases

Bud
375
Methodist
COMPAQ
400
Office DEPOT
375

The "Concrete Doughnuts"

Through the 1960s and 1970s many of the charming old parks of the early century were being traded in for "multipurpose" concrete stadiums, most of which lacked the distinguishing architectural characteristics so common in earlier parks. But starting in the late '60s a new crop of ballparks sprang up that were so similar in design, it was difficult to tell them apart. In a five-year period from 1966 to 1971, cookie-cutter parks popped up in Atlanta, St. Louis, Pittsburgh, Cincinnati, and Philadelphia, all virtually identical. "I stand at the plate," Pirates third baseman Richie Hebner once said of these clones, "and I honestly don't know whether I'm in Pittsburgh, Cincinnati, St. Louis, or Philly. They all look alike."

Dubbed by some as being the dark age of ballparks, the late '60s yielded a crop of stadiums that were a direct affront to baseball's sensibilities. These new parks were a slap in the face of tradition, evidenced by the fact that all of them sported artificial turf when opened (even more amazingly, many of them still do). It's unclear what is more startling about these ball yards: the fact that they are so strikingly similar, or the fact that such heinous mistakes could be so blithely duplicated.

Nicknamed the "concrete doughnuts" for their multilevel oval shapes, these stadiums were considered the future of baseball. Of course, no one could have predicted that a scant twenty-five years later there would be such a backlash against these stadiums that most ball teams would vacate them, and those that didn't would dream of the day when they could.

The infamous troika of "concrete doughnuts." **BELOW:** *Busch Stadium, St. Louis, MO.* **OPPOSITE TOP:** *Three Rivers Stadium in Pittsburgh, PA.* **OPPOSITE BOTTOM:** *Veterans Stadium, Philadelphia, PA.*

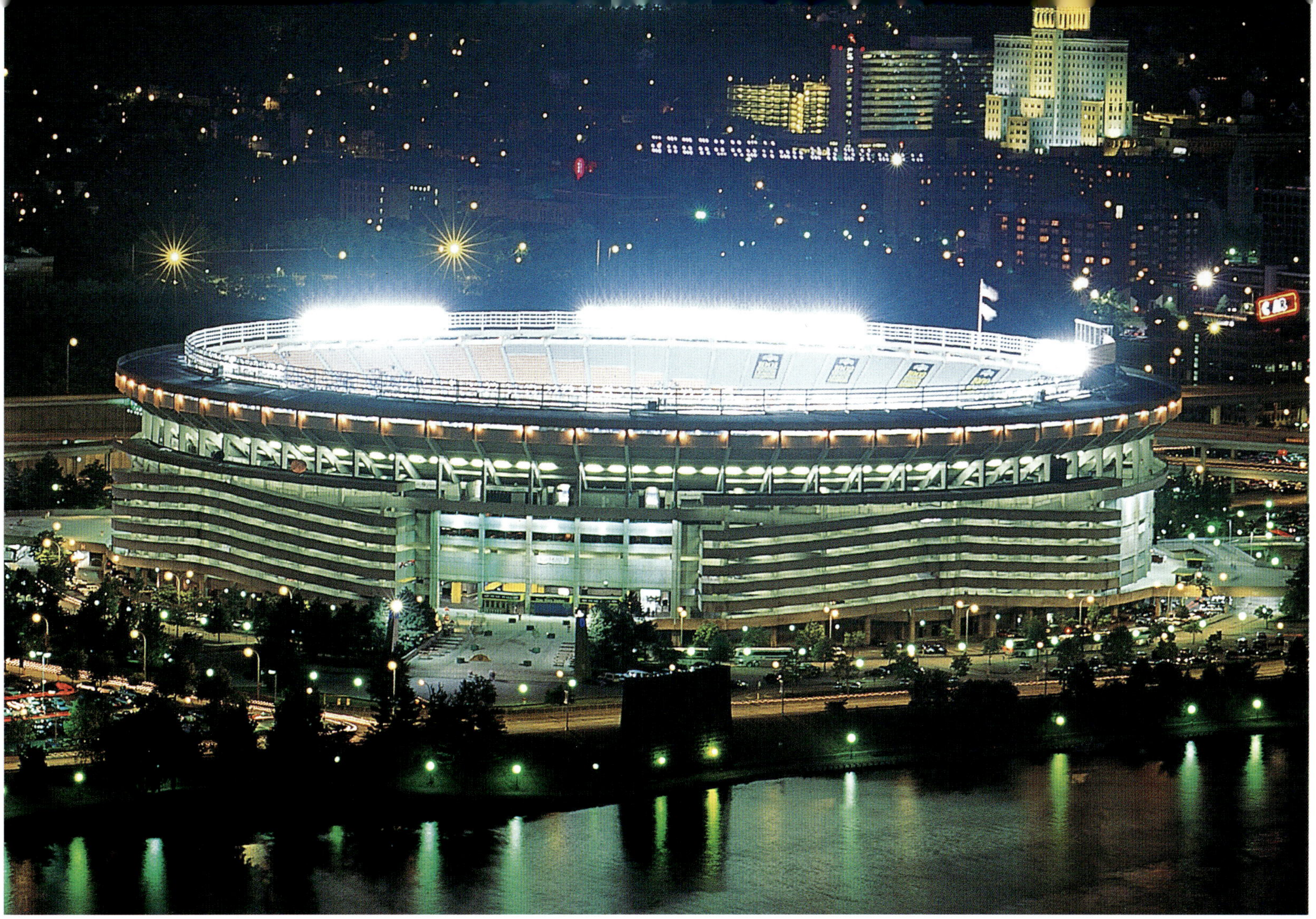

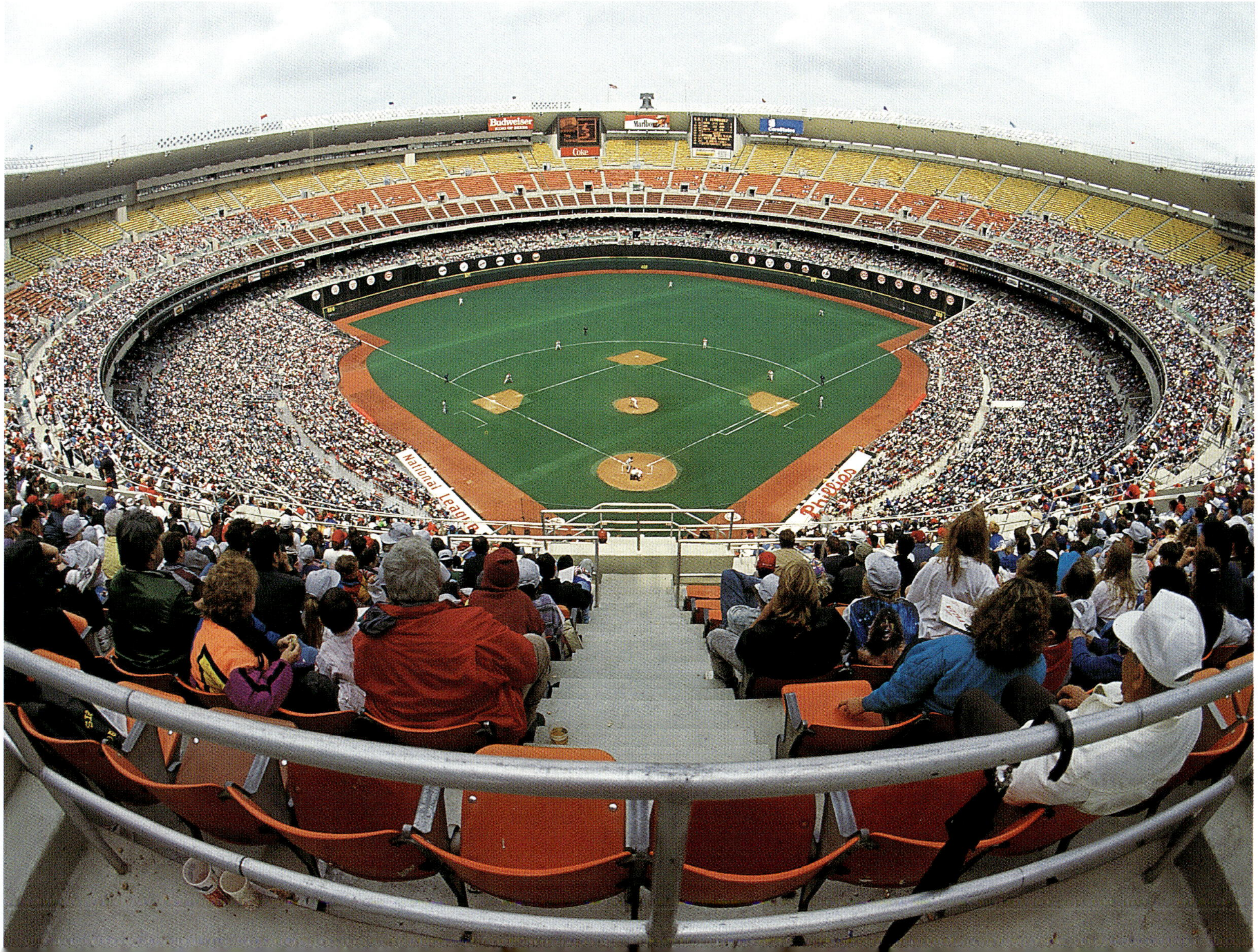
Budweiser
National League
Phillies

ABOVE: *With Mark McGwire breaking records in St. Louis, Cardinal fans have been quite content in Busch Stadium.*
BELOW: *A postcard depicting Sportsman's Park, home of the St. Louis Cardinals from 1920 to 1966.*

Busch Stadium

St. Louis (opened 1966)

Busch Stadium holds the distinction of being the one concrete doughnut with a future. Despite its large capacity and bland architecture, it appears that old St. Louis is relatively satisfied with its concrete oval. With a number of big names in the dugout and historical events unfolding on the field, the Cardinals have done a good job of putting the fans in the seats, which is sure to add longevity to any ballpark.

Sportsman's Park housed the St. Louis Cardinals from 1920 to 1966, and the St. Louis Browns from 1902 until their departure to Baltimore in 1953. By the late 1960s Sportsman's Park was showing its age and the Cardinals started to plan for a new ballpark that was part of a St. Louis downtown rejuvenation project. On May 8, 1966, the Cardinals played their last game at Sportsman's Park—renamed Busch Stadium in 1953 after the beer dynasty that bought the team—and immediately afterward a helicopter transported home plate to the Cardinals new home, also called Busch Stadium.

On May 12, 1966, the Cardinals inaugurated their new ballpark with a twelve-inning win over the Atlanta Braves. Busch Stadium sits within spitting distance of the famous St. Louis arch, and features an arch design of its own along its roof line. A triple-decked concrete marvel, Busch Stadium ushered in a new era of monolith stadiums that were quickly copied, with three nearly identical structures built soon afterward around the country.

Like other parks of the era, Busch Stadium rushed to install artificial turf. But in a unique move, it left the base paths dirt, giving it a more traditional baseball feel. But that didn't last long, and by 1977 the only dirt in Busch stadium was on the dirt "patches" at each base and the pitcher's mound. (Candlestick Park in 1971 was the only other stadium to mix traditional dirt base paths with artificial turf.)

Unlike many of the other cookie-cutter parks, Busch Stadium has seen a rash of improvements over the years. In 1987 every seat was replaced, and the sound and video systems got a big upgrade in 1993. By 1996, Busch Stadium, in a retro upgrade, nixed the wall-to-wall carpeting and went back to a natural playing surface. Adding to that old-time flavor, a hand-operated scoreboard was installed in 1997.

A model of corporate sponsorship, Busch Stadium tinkers with one of the most basic fundamentals of the game. The playing of "Take Me Out to the Ballgame" during the traditional seventh-inning stretch is delayed to the eighth. Instead, the seventh inning is commercial time, a time when the family can sway arm-in-arm to the Anheuser Busch "King of Beers" theme song.

Despite what amounts to a park fans should hate, Busch Stadium has done remarkably well. St. Louis fans, famous for their sports fanaticism, flock to their concrete oval yard in droves. In 1998 Busch Stadium pulled in more than three million fans—an amazing number when you consider that the only National League teams pulling in more (Colorado, Arizona, and Atlanta) all have ballparks built after 1995.

In reality, Busch Stadium's success may have more to do with what baseball affectionately calls "the product" (that is, the players) than with the stadium. In 1997 the Cardinals acquired a stocky first baseman with red hair and a reputation for landing on the disabled list. But it was soon obvious that

Mark McGwire was more than a slugger with Popeye forearms; he was the future of baseball. In 1998 the faithful swarmed through the gates of Busch Stadium to watch McGwire—in a heated contest with the Cubs' Sammy Sosa—take a run at the single-season home run record, and tear it to shreds. By now everyone knows that McGwire knocked out seventy homers in 1998 to break Roger Maris's 1961 record of sixty-one homers. But McGwire also shattered the National League record for most home runs at home (thirty-eight), breaking Ted Kluszewski's 1954 record of thirty-four and ensuring a packed Busch Stadium for the foreseeable future.

The St. Louis skyline and the famous arch peer down over Busch Stadium.

ABOVE: *An archetypal modern-era stadium, Cincinnati's Cinergy Field saw the first World Series on artificial turf in 1970.*

Cinergy Field (formerly Riverfront Stadium)

Cincinnati (opened 1970)

For almost six decades Cincinnati's venerable Crosley Field was the home for the city's Reds. But in the early '60s the old stadium began to show its age in more ways than one. Of course, there were the usual complaints of outdated facilities and small capacity (Crosley held just 29,488 fans). But two important developments spelled the death of Cincinnati's old ballpark.

First was the westward tide that was sweeping baseball teams to the coast. The Dodgers and the Giants were caught up and headed west, and other West Coast cites went fishing for prospects. In the early '60s the city of San Diego lobbied hard for the Reds, offering to build a state-of-the-art ballpark. Having witnessed the demoralization that occurred in New York when two of their three teams left town, Cincinnati was hell-bent not to lose the Reds.

But the death blow to Crosley was professional football, which was growing by leaps and bounds in the '60s. Cincinnati was awarded a professional football franchise in 1966. With that announcement, the city became the next victim of the regrettable trend of multipurpose stadiums, and a new stadium was planned on the Ohio River.

On June 24, 1970, the Reds beat the Giants 5–4 in their last game at Crosley Field, and less than a week later they landed in their spanking-new concrete doughnut. Although it uses the old home plate from Crosley Field, little else of Riverfront Stadium bears much resemblance to traditional ballparks.

Triple-decked all around, Riverfront saw many regrettable firsts. Taking artificial turf to the extreme, Riverfront was the first stadium to carpet the base paths, leaving dirt patches only at the bases, the pitcher's mound, and home plate. Riverfront Stadium also saw the first World Series on artificial turf when the Reds hosted the 1970 fall classic against Baltimore.

The Reds saw many great baseball moments in their concrete tub on the river, including the heyday of the "Big Red Machine" in the 1970s. But with the stratospheric baseball salaries of the '80s and '90s, economic realities took a toll at the ticket booth. In 1998 the Reds ranked twelfth in National League teams in attendance, drawing little more than 22,000 per game at Riverfront, renamed Cinergy Field in the wake of a corporate name sell-off. The boys from Cincinnati visited the World Series four times in the 1970s but appeared only once in the last two decades of the century.

To no one's surprise, the team spent the last years of the twentieth century humping for a new ballpark. With a newly approved ballpark sales tax increase approved in 1996, the Reds put their new ball yard on the fast track. In spring 1999 the Reds signed a thirty-year lease on a new Reds ballpark in Cincinnati, set to open in 2003. Most important for ball fans in town, the lease prohibits the Reds from entering into any agreement to relocate, or even from applying to the National League or Major League Baseball to relocate.

ABOVE: *In the '70s, Riverfront Stadium played host to the Big Red Machine, as the dominating Reds were called, which included Pete Rose (top), and Johnny Bench (bottom).* **LEFT:** *A commemorative belt buckle from Cincinnati's first ballpark, later renamed Crosley Field.*

Three Rivers Stadium

Pittsburgh (opened 1970)

In the late 1960s the Pittsburgh Pirates played ball in Forbes Field, considered small (capacity 35,000) and dilapidated by Pirates owners. Like most teams of the era, the Pirates went looking for a new ballpark. When the adjacent University of Pittsburgh came knocking on the door needing more room, it was enough to get the Pirates into a new home. But the transition wasn't an easy one. Ground breaking took place in April 1968, then construction hit one snag after another. Opening day was delayed in early 1970, then delayed again. Finally, on July 16, 1970, Three Rivers Stadium opened for business.

Remarkably similar to Riverfront Stadium, which opened just two weeks earlier and sits on the same Ohio River, Three Rivers Stadium is named for its vantage point at the intersection of the Allegheny, Monongahela, and Ohio rivers. Like Riverfront before it, this park sports dirt "patches," which the bases and the pitcher's mound peek through. Other than that, it's artificial turf all the way. The outfield is symmetrical and, at 400 feet (122m) in center and 335 feet (102m) at the foul poles, not even long or short enough to be interesting. This lack of character hasn't done much for the turnstiles. In 1998 Pittsburgh pulled in a measly average of 19,512 per game—the second lowest attendance in the National League.

Not surprisingly, Pittsburgh has been looking to take the wrecking ball to Three Rivers Stadium for years. Only four years after a task force was set up to explore a new Pittsburgh ballpark, the Pirates broke ground on a new old-style ballpark to be opened in 2001. Named after the financial services company that will shell out nearly $30 million for the naming rights, PNC Park will be the first ballpark with a two-deck design to be built in the United States since Milwaukee's County Stadium was completed in 1953. With just 38,127 seats, the park will be one of the smallest in the majors, and looks to be a classy reward to all those Pirates fans who endured the years in Three Rivers Stadium.

BELOW: *Like many of the colossal multisport stadiums of the modern era, Three Rivers Stadium has plenty of empty seats these days.*

RIGHT: *The much-loved Forbes Field, home of the Pittsburgh Pirates from 1909 to 1970.* **BELOW:** *A vintage Pirates pennant. The team was nicknamed the Buccaneers, which economical newsmen shortened to "Bucs" to save headline space.*

LEFT: *Pirate great Willie Stargell says good-bye to the faithful at Three Rivers Stadium in 1982.*

LEFT: *Bill Mazeroski is mobbed by fans after his homer in the bottom of the ninth wins the 1960 World Series for the Pirates.*

Veterans Stadium

Philadelphia (opened 1971)

The last of the concrete-doughnut stadiums to come into play, "The Vet" is right at home in the multistadium complex in which it sits. Located right next to the First Union Center and the First Union Spectrum, Veterans Stadium is a large concrete tub among large concrete tubs, and scores a zero for external charm among many baseball fans. "The place looks trashy," remarks author Bob Wood in *Dodger Dogs to Fenway Franks: The Ultimate Guide to America's Top Baseball Parks.* Unfortunately, Wood's critique doesn't improve once he hands over his ticket. "Inside, stadium tackiness intensifies," he writes, noting the park's hideous color scheme.

Veterans Stadium replaced the venerable old Connie Mack Stadium, formerly known as Shibe Park. The first concrete-and-steel stadium in the majors, Shibe Park was constructed in less than a year, typical for the era. Having seen more than sixty years of baseball from both the Philadelphia A's and the Phillies, the old park was starting to show its age by the late '60s. It also had no parking and sat in a decaying neighborhood. So, in 1971, Philadelphia replaced cozy little Connie Mack Stadium with a two-level concrete behemoth that held more than 62,000 fans.

Philly ran into trouble from the start of the project, and cost overruns forced the city to get approval for a second bond issuance in 1967. But the project continued, and on April 4, 1971, a helicopter hovered over the new stadium to throw in the first pitch to Phillies catcher Mike Ryan. Since that time Philly's concrete doughnut has seen three World Series (one successful for the home team, in 1980) and two All-Star games. It also saw some neglect, and in 1994 the Phillies took over management of the yard from the city of Philadelphia.

As for baseball charm, you'll have to look elsewhere. The field is almost a carbon copy of Three Rivers and Riverfront stadiums: artificial turf with dirt patches at the bases and the pitcher's mound. One of the only distinguishing characteristics was a replica Liberty Bell that used to hang from center field,

BELOW: *Phillies infielders (including the great Mike Schmidt on left) play flip at Veterans Stadium before a game in 1974.* **RIGHT:** *Hall of Fame pitcher Steve Carlton spent fifteen years pitching for the Phillies at Veterans Stadium. His number 32, retired for posterity, adorns the outfield wall.*

which was dinged with a home run by Greg Luzinski in 1972.

Unfortunately, the story is the same as at Riverfront and Three Rivers when it comes to long-term success. Attendance at Veterans Stadium is among the lowest in the majors, averaging only 21,718 per game in 1998. With a little luck, Philadelphia hopes soon to follow in Pittsburgh's footsteps and rid itself of its cookie-cutter stadium.

ABOVE: *A night game at Veterans Stadium, 1999.*

LEFT: *Shibe Park was hailed as the crown jewel of ballparks when it opened in 1909. Later renamed Connie Mack Stadium, it was the Phillies' home until 1970.*

PARTIE D'ÉTOILES
MONTRÉAL
1982
ALL-STAR GAME
Montréal
Le 13 juillet 1982
July 13.1982

Olympic Stadium

Montreal (opened 1977)

For the city of Montreal, it seemed the best of plans. First, you acquire a National League expansion franchise with the provision that you will build a domed stadium to house your new team. Then you snag the 1976 Olympic games. You hire a Parisian architect to build an ultra-modern stadium that will house track and field for the '76 Games, and baseball thereafter. To top it all off, the ballpark will be the model for a new generation of retractable-roof parks, allowing open-air baseball in fair weather yet keeping out the Canadian frost on chillier nights. Sounds great, right? Well, two decades and $1 billion later, the Expos now find themselves with a broken-down ballpark and the lowest attendance in the major leagues.

The sad story goes like this: in a major coup for Canada, Major League Baseball awarded an expansion franchise to a group of Montreal businessmen in 1968, creating the first major league baseball team outside the United States. The city christened their new team the Expos after Montreal's "Expo '67" World's Fair, and chose for their home a cozy little municipal stadium called Jarry Park. With a capacity for only 3,000 fans, Jarry Park was quickly renovated, and by opening day of the 1969 season, its capacity was increased to over 28,000. It was nothing fancy, but it did the trick until a new stadium could be built.

Nicknamed the Big O, Olympic Stadium rose like a visitor from outer space in time to host the 1976 Olympic Games. And what an alien it was. Impressively flat with wide support arches flowing down its side, Olympic Stadium was the height of modernism. The structure featured a 556-foot (170m) leaning tower hovering over the stadium, bent auspiciously at a 45-degree angle. Taller than the Washington Monument and leaning nine times steeper than the Leaning Tower of Pisa, the Olympic Stadium tower was at the center of the state-of-the-art retractable-roof system. The tower stood unfinished from

LEFT: *Montreal's billion-dollar Olympic Stadium debuted a wonder of engineering and design, but it has had a hard time keeping its seats full.* **INSET:** *Olympic Stadium hosted the 1982 All-Star game.* **BELOW:** *A head-bobbing Expos souvenir.*

1976 to 1987, and was finally operational in 1989. The massive roof was constructed of more than 60,000 square feet (18,288sq m) of Kevlar, weighing in at a whopping 50 tons. Painted orange on the inside and silver on the exterior, the roof is covered with twenty-six white points that connect it with the tower. Unfortunately, the roof's function never caught up to its style, and many problems were encountered in its operation. It has now remained closed for many seasons, and in January 1999 five people were injured when a panel of the roof gave way under the weight of wet snow.

Olympic Stadium was the first international ballpark. Both the Canadian and the American national anthems are played before every game, and messages on the scoreboard appear in both English and French. A statue of Jackie Robinson stands in the main entrance of Olympic Stadium, a tribute from the city where Robinson got his major league start in the Dodgers' farm system.

The stadium itself stands as a testament to the promises and disappointments of the modern ballpark era. Fluorescent artificial turf covers the field, looked down upon by 46,500 seats with views that are perhaps better suited to track and field than to baseball. All in all, Wrigley Field it ain't.

Through the 1970s, '80s, and '90s, Montreal has built an impressive organization that has been home to a parade of talented young players such as Rusty Staub, Andre Dawson, Tim Wallach, Henry Rodriguez, and Pedro Martinez, only to see them get bought off by deep-pocketed competitors. Without the revenue base to compete, the Expos have never been to the World Series in their entire history.

The Expos and their spaceship stadium found themselves at the end of the twentieth century with the lowest attendance numbers of any major league city. In 1998 the Expos attracted 914,717 fans for the *entire season,* averaging only 11,293 per game.

Like most teams saddled with outdated parks, Montreal has visions of a new ball yard. In June 1997 Expos owners unveiled plans for a new, downtown baseball stadium with a retractable roof. In May 1998 the Expos announced that the new ballpark will be called Labatt Park, after the Canadian Brewery that agreed to pony up $100 million for the naming rights. So it looks like baseball's future in Montreal is secure, for now.

OPPOSITE: *Originally built for the 1976 Olympics, Montreal's "Big O" seems more suited to track and field than to baseball.* **RIGHT:** *Olympic Stadium's space-age retractable roof has remained closed for many seasons.*

347

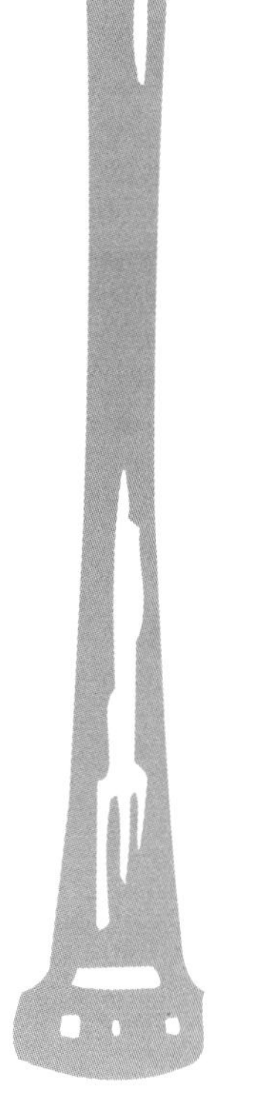

CHAPTER 3

The Revival Era, 1990–present

While it's too early to call the 1990s a golden age of baseball parks, by all indications it might just be one. Between 1990 and 2000, no fewer than twelve new major league ballparks were inaugurated, a trend that continues with two new ballparks in the lineup for opening day 2001. There's no doubt that this last decade of the century will have an enormous impact on what the game will look like in the twenty-first century. There are a slew of reasons why the old parks got the bulldozer, and a lot of them boil down to money and luxury-box revenue. But look deeper, and the real reason lies with the folks in the seats.

OPPOSITE: *The mile-high view from the upper decks of Denver's Coors Field.*

Cozy new stadiums like Jacobs Field in Cleveland have brought back the intimate ballpark experience.

Today, as it did in the years immediately after World War II, baseball once again finds itself mirroring society. When postwar Americans abandoned the cities for the suburbs and hopped off trolleys and into autos, baseball built a generation of monolithic coliseums with sprawling parking lots on the outskirts of town. But as a rejuvenation of American cities began in the 1980s, and the country entered a period of prolonged economic prosperity, people soon got tired of the faceless 'burbs. Style looked backward and anything old became hip, as the Volkswagen Bug made a comeback and Austin Powers swept the United States. Baseball got wise, and saw that its future was in its past.

Toss on your cap and march into one of the new ballparks, and you're struck with a wonderful contradiction. First, many of these ballparks have gone out of their way to adopt the charm of yesteryear's classic parks. The majestic spread of a real grass field is a given, and small baseball-only configurations are the rule of the day. On the other hand, today's new field of dreams is a technological marvel, with big bucks spent

on groundskeeping technology and space-age retractable roofs. While the architects of the '60s and '70s stadiums could be shot for some of the choices they made (we're all still scratching our heads over Astroturf), at least they taught us what *not* to do. Rest assured, today's ballpark builder has learned from past mistakes.

The results are a team of rookie parks that look like Hall of Fame material. Pacific Bell Park, sandwiched in a corner of San Francisco's South of Market district, is a cozy little park with a classic brick exterior that hearkens back to Ebbets Field. Quirky little Jacobs Field in Cleveland not only revitalized a downtown neighborhood, but vaulted the also-ran Indians into perennial pennant threats. And SAFECO Field gave Mariners fans a classic baseball-friendly replacement for the massive Kingdome, while its "umbrella"-style roof combines an open-air vibe with protection from Seattle's inevitable downpours.

There's no guarantee that the new sandlots of today will be the classics of tomorrow. In twenty years we may look back at today's technological marvels and think, "Retractable roofs, what were we thinking?" But judging by the mobs of fans decked out in Orioles jackets streaming into Camden Yards, chances are these new ballparks are a pretty good bet.

The intimate confines of Atlanta's new Turner Field in the foreground contrast sharply with the coldness of Atlanta–Fulton County Stadium in the background.

WELCOME TO
ORIOLE PARK
at
CAMDEN YARDS

Oriole Park at Camden Yards

Baltimore (opened 1992)

By the late 1980s baseball parks were in a pretty sad state of affairs. Many of the old baseball-only parks had been swapped for concrete multipurpose stadiums (as in Pittsburgh, Cincinnati, and Philadelphia) and of the ones that remained, quite a few were getting ready for the wrecking ball (like Tiger Stadium in Detroit and Comiskey Park in Chicago). From an architectural and historical perspective, ballparks were clearly at a crossroads. Many observers of parks clearly asked, "What's next?"

To answer the question, the city of Baltimore stepped up to the plate, and in the process changed the course of ballparks forever. It can be said that no single structure has more greatly affected the history of baseball parks than Oriole Park at Camden Yards. As a throwback to the cozy, intimate confines of yesteryear, Camden Yards ushered in a new era of retro ball yards. With a classic brick facade, intimate seating, and a century-old warehouse looming just beyond center field, Camden Yards has inspired a new generation of parks in almost a dozen cities.

Although Camden Yards has become a symbol of the modern ballpark, its birth arose more out of survival than of trailblazing. Having already lost the football Colts, Baltimore was determined to hang on to their beloved Orioles. Even though the cavernous Memorial Stadium was still in acceptable condition and pulling in around 30,000 fans a game, the city of Baltimore looked for a new park to keep the Orioles in town. The effort got a big boost when the baseball-minded William Donald Schaefer, former mayor of Baltimore, became governor of Maryland and made a new Oriole park a priority. Fortunately, the Orioles simultaneously got a new owner in New York banker Eli Jacobs, a fan of architecture. Together, they pushed for and got a new field.

Construction of Camden Yards began on June 28, 1989. It would be finished in thirty-three months, but before the first ball was thrown out, a name had to be decided on. Schaefer wanted to call the confines Camden Yards after a nineteenth-century Baltimore railway station. Jacobs opted for Oriole Park after the International League park that stood in Baltimore until the '40s. A compromise strung the two names together, and on April 6, 1992, Oriole Park at Camden Yards debuted, with a mouthful of a name now generally truncated to "Camden Yards."

The dimensions of Camden Yards show the influence of the classic parks. Like the late Ebbets Field in Brooklyn, Camden Yards features an asymmetrical outfield, measuring 410 feet (125m) at deepest left-center, 333 feet (101m) in left, and 318 feet (97m) in right. The hitter-friendly dimensions of right field are frustrated by a 25-foot (7.5m) fence, which sports a digital "game in progress" scoreboard. A natural grass surface and steel trusses (rather than concrete) give Camden Yards a wonderfully classic baseball feel. The scoreboard in center field is topped with a vintage-look clock, surrounded by the letters THE SUN, an ad for the local Baltimore newspaper whose H and E light up as a hit/error indicator.

OPPOSITE: *Baltimore's Camden Yards is widely credited with the return of the intimate ballpark* **ABOVE:** *An usher surveys the field at Camden Yards..* **BELOW:** *The Orioles insignia adorns a gate that first swung open on April 6, 1992.*

Nothing gives this park a more metropolitan feel than the immense brick B&O warehouse looming just beyond the right-field wall. Built between 1889 and 1905, the B&O is the largest building on the East Coast, measuring 1,116 feet (340m) long. Today the eight-story brick landmark houses the ballpark's operations and kitchen facilities, as well as the Orioles team office. More than a neighboring building, it is actually part of the game, since the right-field lights hang from the warehouse's roof. It also played a part in a historic countdown in 1995. During that memorable season, numbers soaring 10 feet (3m) high hung from the B&O as Cal Ripken marched toward Lou Gehrig's longstanding record of 2,131 consecutive games played.

Camden Yards sports great sight lines and fantastic seating. But a couple of the seats stand out among the rest. A red seat in left field marks the spot where Cal Ripken landed his 278th homer on July 15, 1993, surpassing Ernie Banks for most home runs hit by a shortstop. And in the right-field bleachers, look for a special seat that marks the landing of Eddie Murray's 500th home run, which he dinged on September 6, 1996, to become only the fifteenth player to reach the 500 club.

When most fans think of Babe Ruth they think of New York, and perhaps Boston. But Camden Yards is steeped in Ruth history. Ruth started his career with the minor league Orioles, who signed him for a paltry $600 in 1914. Unfortunately, the struggling Orioles had to sell the Babe, who went to the Red Sox for five seasons before becoming a legendary Yankee. The birthplace of the Bambino is just blocks away, and today a 9-foot (2.7m) bronze statue of Ruth sits at the entrance near the north end of the warehouse. Center field at Camden Yards is now a patch of majestic grass, but it was once the site of the saloon owned by Ruth's father.

ABOVE: *Ticket to the 1958 All-Star game held at Memorial Stadium, home of the Orioles from 1954 to 1991.* **BELOW:** *The "Iron Man," Cal Ripken, who broke Lou Gehrig's record for consecutive games played by stringing together 2,632.* **OPPOSITE:** *Camden Yards, where every seat is in on the action.*

Jacobs Field

Cleveland (opened 1994)

Cleveland's Jacobs Field is one of the most perfect ballparks in baseball. After spending many long years in the cold, cavernous Cleveland Stadium (dubbed "The Mistake by the Lake"), the Indians deserve Jacobs Field. So dramatic was the move that writer Ed Sherman called the switch "like moving from Siberia to Maui."

Along with Camden Yards in Baltimore, Jacobs Field has become synonymous with the return of open-air, natural-grass ballparks. Seating just over 43,000, Jacobs Field is a snug little park located right in the heart of Cleveland. No doubt about it, this joint was designed with the fan in mind. Seats are generous in width and angled toward the playing field. With the Cleveland skyline looming in the background, the park sports a quirky, asymmetrical playing field and natural-grass playing surface.

Left field ends at a 19-foot (5.8m) "mini monster" (nicknamed in deference to the infamous Green Monster at Boston's Fenway Park), complete with game-in-progress scoreboard. In a throwback to old parks, the scoreboard in left field is plastered with advertisements.

BELOW: *The return to natural-grass fields is a hallmark of today's retro ballparks.* **RIGHT:** *Jacobs Field has been one of the most consistently sold-out ballparks in the history of baseball.*

JACOBS FIELD
HOME OF THE
CLEVELAND
Indians
MAIN CONCOURSE

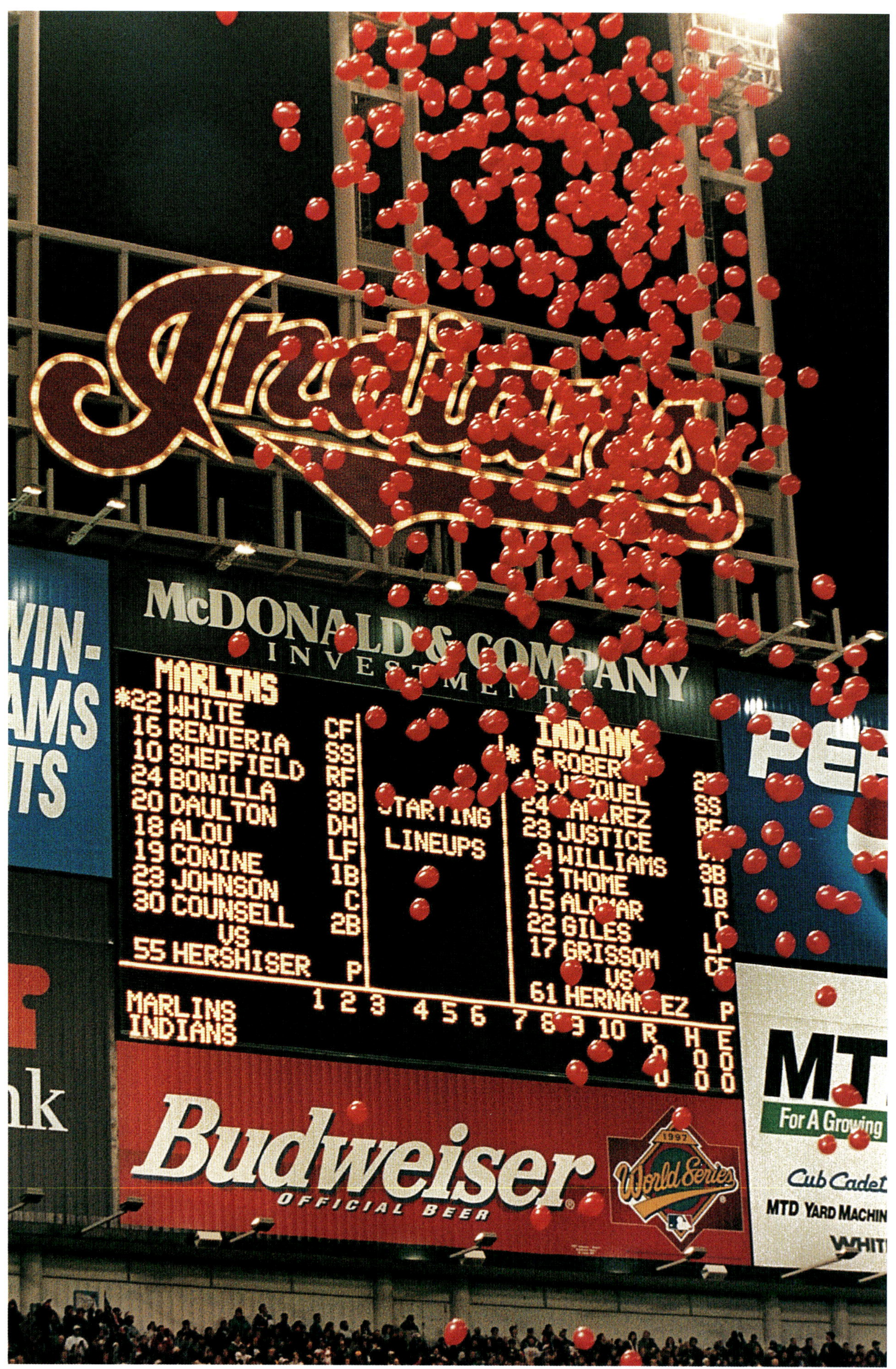
Indians
McDONALD
INVEST
MARLINS
*22 WHITE
16 RENTERIA CF
10 SHEFFIELD SS
24 BONILLA RF
20 DAULTON 3B
18 ALOU DH
19 CONINE LF
23 JOHNSON 1B
30 COUNSELL C
VS 2B
55 HERSHISER P
LINEUPS
23 JUSTICE
WILLIAMS
THOME 3B
GILES
17 GRISSOM
VS
MARLINS 1 2 3 4 5 6 7 8 9 10 R H E
INDIANS
Budweiser
OFFICIAL BEER
1997
World Series
For A Growing
Cub Cadet

It's no coincidence that as soon as the Indians took up residence in Jacobs Field they shot to the top of the Central Division of the American League—increased revenue from all those sold-out games bought quality players. Before the construction of Jacobs Field, the Indians hadn't seen a pennant since 1954. In the new yard, the boys from Cleveland have been to the fall classic twice, in 1995 and 1997.

In Jacobs Field, almost everything is a mixture of old charm and modern reality. Even the name is a hybrid of old and new. In the early part of the twentieth century, ballparks were named after powerful owners, like Wrigley Field, Comiskey Park, and Ebbets Field. Nowadays the corporation reigns supreme, and even the name above the turnstile isn't immune to corporate money. Witness the large sums paid just for the naming rights to Pacific Bell Park, SAFECO Field, Coors Field, and Comerica Park. Jacobs Field gets its moniker from Richard Jacobs, the Indians owner who fought so hard to keep baseball in Cleveland. But it wasn't all sentimental: Jacobs also forked over $13 million for the naming rights.

Of course, this is 1990s baseball, and fan comforts notwithstanding, the real benchmarks of a ballpark's success are at the ticket booth. In this respect, it appears the Indians are knocking it out of the park. In 1996, before a single inning had been played, the Indians sold out the entire season, an unprecedented feat made more amazing by the fact that they had repeat preseason sellouts in 1997, 1998, and 1999! In fact, while the novelty of a new ballpark is quickly wearing off in places like Chicago, the honeymoon is far from over in Cleveland. The average attendance at Jacobs Field in 1998 was more than 42,000, their highest ever. Compare this with the pathetic numbers at Cleveland Stadium, which held more than 74,000 fans per game but averaged fewer than 26,000 in 1993.

OPPOSITE: *Jacobs Field erupts with postseason fervor during the 1997 World Series.* **ABOVE:** *The perennially empty Cleveland Stadium, home to the Indians from 1932 to 1993, was widely lamented as "The Mistake by the Lake."* **INSERT:** *Collectible Indians scorecard.*

SOUTHWEST
MRS BAIRD'S BREAD
WELLS FARGO
QualityCare Network
BUD LIGHT
Coca-Cola
39
Bud
TARGET
TARGET
The New Dodge
BUD LIGHT
Sports Day

Ballpark in Arlington

Arlington, Texas (opened 1994) The Ballpark in Arlington is part modern stadium, part retro ballpark, and part amusement park. It went up in just twenty-three months at a cost of $191 million, and saw its first game on April 1, 1994. This modern gem is located right next to Six Flags Over Texas, a 200-acre (80ha) amusement park.

The Ballpark in Arlington replaced Arlington Stadium, the field which had been the home of the Texas Rangers for twenty-two years. Originally named Turnpike Stadium, Arlington Stadium housed a number of minor league teams from Dallas and Fort Worth in its cozy 10,000-seat confines. When the Washington Senators decided to move to Texas for the 1972 season, the park changed its name and tripled in capacity to welcome its new major league team. But after two decades, the old stadium had outlived its usefulness, and a new stadium was planned for the 1994 season.

LEFT: *The Ballpark in Arlington features a right-field "porch" reminiscent of that of the late Tiger Stadium.* **ABOVE:** *Texas Ranger catcher Ivan Rodriguez goes over the rail fielding a foul ball in the Ballpark in Arlington in 1998.*

ABOVE: *The Ballpark in Arlington: part modern stadium, part retro ballpark, and part amusement park.* **RIGHT:** *Hall of Fame hurler Nolan Ryan, who had two no-hitters as a Texas Ranger.*

The new Ballpark in Arlington is a jewel of a ballpark, with a retro red granite and brick exterior. Two large brick towers welcome visitors, and the archway features thirty-five steer heads and twenty-one lone stars cast out of stone. A brick "Walk of Fame" rings the entire perimeter of the ballpark, and tells the story of the Texas Rangers from their birth in 1971.

One thing's for sure: this ain't your grandfather's ballpark. Inside the amenities really begin. The Ballpark in Arlington features the Legends of the Game Baseball Museum, a 17,000-square-foot (5181sq m) exhibit with a 225-seat theater; a picnic area just beyond center field, an art gallery beyond that, and a children's learning center. In case that wasn't enough, they decided to create a 12-acre (4.8ha) lake right next door.

Not to be lost among the amenities is an actual baseball park, which sports some quirky asymmetrical outfield dimensions. One of the unique features of the park is a two-tiered home run porch in right field, modeled after the design made famous at Detroit's Tiger Stadium—but this one is tailored for Texas weather, with ceiling fans whirring away overhead.

It's a combination that the Texans seem to love. In 1998 the Ballpark in Arlington ranked third in the American League in attendance, averaging 36,141 fans per game.

The brick facades of today's ballparks hearken back to the days of Ebbets Field and other classic sandlots.

Coors Field

Denver (opened 1995)

Along with Camden Yards and Jacobs Field, Coors Field is one of the "crown jewel" baseball yards credited with the revival of the old-time ballpark. This majestic sandlot sits in a previously industrial section of downtown Denver known as "LoDo." One expansion team and $215 million later, the area has now become a mecca for baseball fans, and no tour of baseball parks would be complete without some time at Coors Field.

Coors Field is an almost perfect mix of old and new. The ballpark itself sits on the site of Denver's first railroad station, Denver Pacific Depot, and its magnificent architecture is right at home in the neighborhood. The exterior is hand-laid brick, and the main entrance is topped by an old-fashioned clock tower. The words COORS FIELD spelled out in shiny silver letters greet the visitor upon entry. And even though the diamond is kept immaculately snow-free by an advanced heating system below the surface, it is still looked upon by a manual scoreboard in right field.

Coors Field has been known as a hitter's park from the day it opened. The foul territory at Coors Field is among the smallest in baseball, with about 56 feet (17m) between home plate and the first row—good for fans trying to get close to the game, bad for pitchers looking for

RIGHT: *The majestic entrance to Coors Field, considered one of the most intimate professional ballparks in the country.*

BELOW: *A Colorado Rockies pennant.*

BULOVA
FIELD

MELODY HOMES
850 KOA

the quick foul out. But the biggest foe a pitcher has in Denver is the altitude. The thin mountain air reportedly allows hits to coast 9 percent farther. The result: lots of four-baggers. In 1998 there were only three games played in Coors Field without a home run. Since opening, the park has seen eight games with more than eight dingers, the record being an astonishing ten home runs during a 1996 slugfest with the Dodgers (the Rockies ultimately won 16–15). In case you're not sure just how high up the park is, just check out the upper deck. Six rows from the top, you'll find a row of purple seats, marking the precise mile-high point, 5,280 feet (1609m) above sea level.

In terms of charm, amenities, and excitement, Coors Field ranks among the top in baseball parks. But in attendance, this ballpark stands alone. The Rockies' yard was originally designed to seat 43,800, but in 1993 Rockies owners saw their expansion team pack Mile High Stadium in their inaugural season, setting a major league single-season attendance record of 4,483,350. This sent them scurrying back to the drawing board, bringing Coors Field up to its current capacity of 50,381. Since moving out of Mile High, Colorado has consistently been a top draw among the majors. In 1998 the Rockies drew 3,789,347 fans, the most in the majors, averaging more than 46,000 per game. With these kinds of numbers as a yardstick, you can bet other major league cities are looking to duplicate the success of Coors Field.

LEFT: *The view from the outfield at Denver's Coors Field. Today's new ballparks are not only popular with fans, but players too.*

Bank One Ballpark

Phoenix (opened 1998)

With an endless parade of amenities, Bank One Ballpark shocked purists when it opened in 1998.

When Bank One Ballpark opened its doors on March 31, 1998, there was no denying that ballparks had entered a whole new era. Nicknamed BOB and costing a whopping $356 million to build, this glitzy oasis shocked baseball purists, who saw its endless parade of amusements as a distraction from the grand old game. But whether you like it or not, there's no denying that Bank One Ballpark is a window into the future of ballparks. Get used to it.

From the outside, it's difficult to tell if Bank One Ballpark is a retro-style ballpark or a warehouse. With an exterior of red brick and green structural steel, it looks like a mixture of both. The most distinctive feature of Bank One is a massive retractable roof that helps shield fans from the brutal Arizona heat. The ballpark's roof is comprised of nine million pounds (4.1 million kg) of steel, and can be opened in less than five minutes by a pair of 200–horsepower motors. The unique roof allows for what is called "sun tracking," which involves adjusting the roof for maximum sun on the field and maximum shade on the seats. The park also sports a massive air-conditioning system, which can bring the temperature down by 30°F (about 18°C) in just three hours.

As for the amenities, it's difficult to know where to start. Within its humble walls, Bank One Ballpark features a two-story baseball museum and a massive multimedia baseball exhibit with 130 monitors. For those who are hungry, the park has an incredible quarter mile (.4km) of concession stands, as well as a number of specialty stands, including a farmer's market. No one goes thirsty here, with an on-site microbrewery and two 6,000-square-foot (1829sq m) beer gardens. But the most extravagant amenity of all is the Sun Pool Party Pavilion, located a few feet from the action beyond the wall in right-center field. Up to thirty-five people can book the pavilion and field homers from the pool; the only thing between them and the fielders is a see-through home run wall.

Seating was a major priority when designing BOB, and more than 80 percent of the seats are inside the foul poles. Seats are extra wide, and there's a cup holder at every seat. And as baseball enters an era of polarity, where the cheap

seats are really cheap and the swanky boxes cost a fortune, this ballpark leads the way. For those on a budget (and with good hiking shoes), the ultra-steep upper-level seats are dirt cheap. At the other end of the spectrum, the well-heeled get pampered in the Diamond Level, with access to a swanky private club that is the equal of anything in Hollywood.

But considering all the money and attention put into this high-tech field, a singular symbol of baseball simplicity somehow found its way into the design. In a rare throwback to yesteryear, Bank One Ballpark sports a dirt path between the pitcher's mound and home plate, a charming feature not seen in a major league park in decades.

ABOVE: *BOB's high-tech retractable roof is comprised of nine million pounds of steel.* **RIGHT:** *The Diamondbacks are a team that spares no expense on their ballpark or on their star players, like the pricey Randy Johnson.*

ABOVE: *Seattle superstar Ken Griffey, Jr.* **RIGHT:** *Fireworks light up the cap of the Kingdome, the Mariner's domed home until 1999.*

SAFECO Field

Seattle (opened 1999)

Let it not be said that the road to revival is cheap. In 1997, after spending twenty years playing on the Astroturf of the football-friendly Kingdome, the Seattle Mariners began a journey toward a new state-of-the-art ballpark. The fare for the road trip: a whopping $517 million. With a tab final for the stadium and surrounding projects costing $100 million above original estimates, SAFECO Field now stands as the most expensive American baseball stadium project of the twentieth century.

SAFECO Field is one of the most technologically advanced ballparks in the country. Located a stone's throw from the Kingdome in downtown Seattle, the Mariners' new ballpark is a hybrid of the best of the old ballparks and state-of-the-art technology. The ballpark holds a baseball-friendly 47,000 people, and features a real grass field. But to see the true innovations made at SAFECO, you have to look literally high and low.

SAFECO Field is one of a new generation of retractable-roof ball fields. Given Seattle's perennially soggy climate, this is understandable. But what makes this park unique is its

retractable "umbrella"-style roof. While most stadiums with retractable roofs close the lid as tight as a mayonnaise jar, SAFECO's roof simply covers the stadium. This allows protection from the elements, yet still provides an open-air feeling. The roof is made of three panels that span railroad tracks, which can be rolled closed in 10–20 minutes, even when games are in progress. The massive roof weighs in at about 11,000 tons and contains enough steel to build a fifty-five-story skyscraper.

SAFECO has a few clever tricks to offer under foot, as well. There used to be a day when growing a grass playing field meant tossing some seed on the ground and watering it. But SAFECO Field has taken the art of groundskeeping to new heights, or more appropriately, depths. Below the surface at SAFECO Field lies one of the most complicated infrastructures of any field. More than 20 miles (32km) of one-inch (2.54cm) plastic hose is snaked below the playing surface. Warm water circulating through the hoses can warm the playing surface to 50–65°F (10–18°C), which compensates for lack of sunlight and helps fool the grass out of dormancy about three months early in the spring.

The Seattle Mariners tip their caps during the National Anthem on opening day at SAFECO Field on July 15, 1999.

Enron Field

Houston (opened 2000)

After thirty-one years of slugging it out in the Astrodome, in 1996 the Houston Astros had had enough of their space-age ballpark. With other cities using revenue from swanky new ballparks to build championship teams, the Astros jumped on the new-stadium bandwagon. After the Houston Oilers left for Tennessee, Houston realized that the threat of sports teams leaving town was more than idle, and the momentum for a new ballpark picked up steam.

Looking to duplicate the successes in Baltimore and Cleveland, Astros owner Drayton McLane, Jr., pushed to build a downtown ballpark, reversing the suburban migration of ballparks that started in the 1960s. In 1995 McLane came close to selling the team to Virginia businessmen who wanted a ball team for suburban Washington, D.C. But in late 1996 the voters of Harris County approved a new ballpark. Ground breaking on the new park, which was to be called the Ballpark at Union Station, occurred on October 30, 1997.

An intimate stadium holding 42,000 fans, the stadium sports a natural-surface playing field and a classic brick facade. Playing summer ball in Houston can be a humid affair, but many fans found the perennially air-conditioned Astrodome to be too artificial a substitute. Today's Astros look to have it both ways with a massive, state-of-the-art retractable roof allowing an open-air baseball field on days that permit it. Built to withstand a hurricane, the roof will open and close in twelve minutes, and do so efficiently. The cost of the roof is estimated at $65 million, with energy costs estimated at just $5 per usage. The roof is expected to roll open about eighty times a year, traveling 14.6 miles (23km) over its transport tracks annually. Estimated life expectancy: 50 years or 730 miles (1175km).

The Astros' new ballpark is more than a great new home for America's pastime; it's insurance against the Astros skipping town, since they've signed a thirty-year lease on the new yard. And while the new Houston ballpark is designed to be a bit of a throwback stylistically, it is cutting edge in its business arrangements. In April 1999 the Astros penned a thirty-year "integrated naming rights agreement" with Enron Energy Services. Estimated to be worth $100 million, the pact gives Enron the naming rights but also allows them to provide service for heating, ventilation, and air-conditioning.

An aerial view of Houston's Enron Field during the contruction process. The stadium, now complete, is slated to open for the 2000 season.

LEFT: *The Astros hope a revamped stadium with a retractable roof will help draw more fans to home games than did the outdated Astrodome.*

Pacific Bell Park

San Francisco (opened 2000)

After spending more than thirty years in Candlestick Park, the San Francisco Giants by 1996 were in a tough way. The team was losing money, and fans were universally rejecting their frigid wind tunnel of a ballpark. Just three years earlier, things had looked much rosier. Led by Safeway chairman and CEO Peter Magowan, a group of local businesspeople had bought the club and saved it from an exodus to Florida. They scooped up superstar free agent Barry Bonds, and built a solid team that came within one game of winning the 1993 division title. Not only that, it looked like they had enough momentum to get a new stadium built in the city of San Francisco, which most observers agreed was the key to the Giants' long-term viability.

But getting a new park was no easy task. San Francisco voters rejected funding for a new stadium four times, demonstrating a brand of shallow-pocketed thrift the *Wall Street Journal* later called "voter fatigue." Giants owners decided to try another route. In December 1995 the team unveiled plans for a nice little downtown park, located in San Francisco's South of Market district. This little gem of a ballpark was everything Candlestick Park wasn't: small and cozy, with classic architectural features and, most of all, better weather. But its best feature was the financial cost to the city. Total amount of public money needed for direct construction: $0.

The Giants envisioned paying for their ballpark by selling most parts of it, including the name itself. In addition, the team would market an aggressive number of "charter seat licenses," basically the right to buy season tickets. Overall the plan was for corporations and season-ticket holders—not the general public—to carry the financial load. It was a formula for the '90s, and in March 1996 voters took the bait, approving the construction of the first privately funded ballpark since Dodger Stadium in 1962. In April 1996 the Giants announced they had sold the name to Pacific Bell, a local phone company, and the new yard was dubbed Pacific Bell Park.

Everything about this park is designed to be a mix of new and old. The Giants' new ballpark

OPPOSITE: *One of the first things to go up in San Francisco's new park was home plate.* **LEFT:** *Pacific Bell Park under construction on the edge of San Francisco Bay in June 1999.*

It was cold, windy, and foggy and many fans were ready to vacate the Giants' first San Francisco home . . .

is squeezed into a 13-acre (5.2ha) site against the San Francisco Bay, and seats just 41,000. Designed by HOK Sport, the same firm responsible for Camden Yards and Jacobs Field, Pacific Bell Park sports a classic brick facade that fits in perfectly with the warehouses of this once-industrial part of the city. The small amount of foul territory creates intimate seating reminiscent of Ebbets Field, and the seats themselves are extra wide and angled toward home plate.

This park even takes into account one of the most important but widely neglected amenities in stadiums: bathrooms. Pacific Bell Park has been designed to achieve "potty parity." Equitable bathroom accommodations are provided for men and women by taking into account the "differences" in bathroom habits among the sexes, all in an effort to make a more "bladder-friendly" park.

Pacific Bell Park is tucked right up against San Francisco Bay and, like many of its urban predecessors, its irregular dimensions result from being sandwiched into an urban neighborhood. But in this park the water is not just a spectator, it plays backup to the right fielder. With the right-field fence only 307 feet (94m) from home plate, dingers regularly land in the bay. This tradition of soggy four-baggers started on December 11, 1997, when the Giants celebrated ground breaking by watching Barry Bonds knock a ball into the bay from the roof of a soon-to-be-demolished warehouse. Just beyond the right-field wall, along the water, a promenade allows passersby to watch the game through the fence.

Every inch of Pacific Bell Park is designed with a reverence for the past, an impression that greets the visitor from the front door. The entire entrance to the park on Third and King streets is a tribute to Willie Mays, one of the greatest players ever to wear a Giants uniform. A statue of Mays in the midst of a monster swing stands at the entrance to the park, surrounded by twenty-four palm trees in honor of the number the "Say Hey Kid" wore as a Giant. Even the park's mailing address, 24 Willie Mays Plaza, honors the slugger.

Without a doubt, the biggest change from Candlestick Park to Pacific Bell Park is the weather. The Giants' old park was famous for its hurricane gusts that made playing the outfield a high-wire act. For fans, a day at Candlestick was a frigid affair, and wool mittens were standard baseball attire. So it's not surprising that the designers of Pacific Bell Park worked overtime to shield players and fans from the hearty San Francisco winds. By all accounts they succeeded beautifully. Pacific Bell Park is located in one of the sunniest parts of the city, and the ballpark was specifically designed to reduce wind. The result: while the wind may be howling at the Willie Mays statue on Third Street, the air at home plate wouldn't move a peanut wrapper. In fact, the design is so successful that Giants coach Sonny Jackson thinks the team may lose home field advantage. "The only bad thing about it is people are going to enjoy coming here to play," Jackson said in 1999. "Now [at Candlestick Park], people hate coming here and playing because of the wind. That's been to our advantage."

More than just a fun place to spend an afternoon, Pacific Bell Park and the other new ballparks around the country are leading a revitalization of American urban centers, reversing years of decay and neglect brought on by a defection to the suburbs. In many ways the game of baseball and the plight of American cities have gone hand in hand. As the urban streets of America became a grimy mess, with shuttered storefronts and dangerous streets, families stayed away, and so did ballparks. But the resulting solution of sterile, concrete suburban stadiums wasn't the answer either.

Today, both baseball and America's cities have reasons to celebrate. The most optimistic among us like to say that landing a new ballpark in a forsaken part of the city is a solid reminder of how our country once was, when bustling city streets overflowed with buoyant baseball fans. The more pessimistic say it's all about money, and cry that corporate-named ballparks are little more than customer-fleecing machines looking to charge $6 for a beer. But there's an easy end to this debate, and it comes right out of Business 101: listen to your customers. And the jury is most definitely in. If the legions of patrons streaming into Pacific Bell Park are any indication, these new ballparks are filling a great need not only in American cities, but in the hearts of baseball fans everywhere.

. . . but others felt a bit more sentimental about the Giants' last game in their old stadium.

ABOVE: *County Stadium, the home of the Brewers until Miller Park is complete, has the unique distinction of being the only stadium with a beer keg in center field.*

Miller Park

Milwaukee
(scheduled to open 2001)

For almost thirty years the Milwaukee Brewers have played ball in County Stadium, a bland municipal ballpark as nondescript as its name. In many ways County Stadium was as much of a hand-me-down as the team itself. The Brewers rose out of the ashes of the Seattle Pilots, an expansion franchise that lasted a single season before a group of Wisconsin businessmen brought the team to Milwaukee in 1970. To house their new team, the owners looked to put County Stadium back in commission. The yard was the home of the Milwaukee Braves from 1953 until their exit in 1965, when they left town for Atlanta. By 1999 the Brewers had almost three decades in County Stadium, and many said that a new ballpark was long overdue. But unfortunately for the Brewers and the city of Milwaukee, the road to a new stadium has not been an easy one.

Ironically, for a town as deserving of a new stadium as Milwaukee, the problems with Miller Park started almost immediately after ground breaking. The Brewers' new park was originally scheduled to open in 1999, and the team had pulled a coup by snagging the 1999 All-Star game. But financing snags delayed construction, and opening day was pushed back, sending the All-Star game to Fenway Park in Boston.

By the summer of 1999 construction of Miller Park was progressing swimmingly until trouble hit again, and this time the consequences were tragic. On July 14, 1999, strong winds toppled a large crane as it was hoisting a piece of the park's retractable roof into place. The resulting accident killed three construction workers and seriously damaged the park, destroying two of the seven roof panels that were already in place and damaging a large portion of the concrete seating bowl below.

Sadly, the deaths at Miller Park hearken back to a similar tragedy that occurred during the construction at County Stadium. From 1950 to 1952, three workers also were killed during stadium construction; one was struck by a fallen beam and two others were killed when a bucket they were in fell to the ground.

The 1999 accident, which was blamed on "ground failure," threw another wrench into the Brewers' plans to begin the 2000 season in a brand-new park. But as of this writing, construction continues, and Miller Park is set to see its first pitch on opening day in 2001. At a total cost of about $400 million, Miller Park will sport all the characteristics of today's breed of retro parks. The yard will feature an asymmetrical outfield, natural-grass playing surface, and extra-wide seats angled toward home plate. Amenities will abound, and in this beer capital of America, it goes without saying that there will be a microbrewery on the premises.

The new Brewers' park will stand in stark contrast to the antiquated tin-can look of County Stadium. Located about 100 feet (30m) directly southeast of the old park, Miller Park will feature a towering, arched retractable-roof system designed to keep out the Midwest rain and cold. The state-of-the-art roof, which will open like a fan in about ten minutes, will weigh 12,000 tons and at its tallest point measure 330 feet (100m) above ground, more than three times the height of the adjacent County Stadium.

Most modern ballparks struggle to accommodate the well-heeled patrons in the box seats yet not price out the families in the bleachers. To achieve this parity, the spread in prices at Miller Park is wider than any center-field gap. Among its four levels of seating, Miller Park has more than fifteen different ticket prices. For the swank set, the Field Diamond Box seats in the first five rows put you right in the action, to the tune of $50 per seat. At the other end of the spectrum, you can get a seat for a buck, but there's a catch. Because of the massive workings of the retractable roof, some 200 to 300 seats

will have obstructed views. Dubbed "Uecker Seats" after radio broadcaster and baseball funnyman Bob Uecker (who was banished to the nosebleed seats in a popular Miller Lite commercial in the 1980s), they will sell for $1 on the day of the game.

ABOVE: *The construction of Miller Park, which was delayed due to a tragic accident that killed three workers, looms large over County Stadium.* **LEFT:** *A 1957 World Series ticket featuring the Milwaukee Braves, the only Wisconsin team ever to win the fall classic.*

APPENDIX

Major League Ballparks: Selected Statistics through 1999

Note: All outfield dimensions given are current as of 1999; in the case of defunct parks, final dimensions are provided.

Arizona

Bank One Ballpark
Phoenix, AZ
401 E. Jefferson Street, PO Box 2095,
Phoenix, AZ 85001
(602) 514-8500
Home Team: Arizona Diamondbacks
Opening Date: March 31, 1998
Capacity: 48, 569
Outfield Dimensions: LF 330 feet (100.6m); CF 407 feet (124.1m); RF 334 feet (101.8m)
Turf: Auza Grass (1998); Kentucky Bluegrass (1999)

California

Edison International Field
Anaheim, CA
2000 Gene Autry Way,
Anaheim, CA 92806
(888) 796-4256
Home Team: Anaheim Angels
Opening Date: April 19, 1966
Capacity (Original; Latest): 43,000 (1996); 45,050 (1998)
Outfield Dimensions: LF 330 feet (100.6m); CF 406 feet (123.7m); RF 330 feet (100.6m)
Turf: Bluegrass

Dodger Stadium
Los Angeles, CA
1000 Elysian Park Avenue,
Los Angeles, CA 90012
(323) 224-1400; Tickets (323) 224-1HIT
Home Team: Los Angeles Dodgers
Opening Date: April 10, 1962
Capacity: 56, 000
Outfield Dimensions: LF 330 feet (100.6m); CF 395 feet (120.4m); RF 330 feet (100.6m)
Turf: Santa Ana Bermuda Grass

Network Associates Coliseum (formerly Oakland-Alameda County Coliseum)
Oakland, CA
7000 Coliseum Way,
Oakland, CA 94621
(510) 638-4900
Home Team: Oakland Athletics
Opening Date: April 17, 1968
Capacity (Original; Latest): 50,000 (1968); 48,219 (1996)
Outfield Dimensions: LF 330 feet (100.6m); CF 400 feet (121.9m); RF 330 feet (100.6m)
Turf: Bluegrass

Qualcomm Stadium
San Diego, CA
9449 Friars Road,
San Diego, CA 92108
(619) 452-SEAT
Home Team: San Diego Padres
Opening Date: August 20, 1967
Capacity (Original; Latest): 50, 000 (1957); 67,544 (1997)
Outfield Dimensions: LF 327 feet (99.7m); CF 405 feet (123.4m); RF 330 feet (100.6m)
Turf: Santa Ana Bermuda Grass

3Com Park (formerly Candlestick Park)
San Francisco, CA
3Com Park,
San Francisco, CA 94124
(415) 467-8000
Home Team: San Francisco Giants
Opening Date: April 12, 1960
Last Baseball Game: September 30, 1999
Capacity (Original; Latest): 43,765 (1960); 58,000 (1993)
Outfield Dimensions: LF 335 feet (102.2m); CF 365 feet (111.3m); RF 328 feet (99.9m)
Turf: Bluegrass (1960); Artificial (1971); Bluegrass (1979)

Colorado

Coors Field
Denver, CO
2001 Blake Street,
Denver, CO 80205
(303) ROCKIES
Home Team: Colorado Rockies
Opening Date: April 26, 1995
Capacity (Original; Latest): 50,200 (1995); 50,381 (1999)
Outfield Dimensions: LF 347 feet (105.8m); CF 445 feet (135.6m); RF 350 feet (106.7m)
Turf: Grass

Florida

Pro Player Stadium (formerly Joe Robbie Stadium)
Miami, FL
2269 N.W. 199th Street,
Miami, FL 33056
(305) 626-7400
Home Team: Florida Marlins
Opening Date: August 16, 1987; first Marlins game: April 5, 1993
Capacity: 47,662
Outfield Dimensions: LF 335 feet (102.2m); CF 404 feet (123.1m); RF 345 feet (105.2m)
Turf: Tifway 419 Bermuda Grass

Tropicana Field
St. Petersburg, FL
1 Stadium Drive, St.
Petersburg, FL 33705
(888) 326-7297
Home Team: Tampa Bay Devil Rays
Opening Date: March 3, 1990; first Devil Rays game: March 31, 1998
Capacity: 45,000
Outfield Dimensions: LF 315 feet (96m); CF 404 feet (123.1m); RF 322 feet (98.1m)
Turf: Astroturf with dirt infield

Georgia

Turner Field
Atlanta, GA
755 Hank Aaron Drive,
Atlanta, GA 30302
(404) 522-7630
Home Team: Atlanta Braves
Opening Date: March 29, 1997
Capacity: 49,831
Outfield Dimensions: LF 335 feet (102.1m); CF 401 feet (122.2m); RF 330 feet (100.6m)
Turf: GN-1 Bermuda Grass

Illinois

Comiskey Park
Chicago, IL
Home Team: Chicago White Sox
Opening Date: July 1, 1910
Last Game: September 30, 1990
Capacity (Original; Latest): 32,000 (1910); 52,000 (1927)
Outfield Dimensions: LF 362 feet (110.3m); CF 420 feet (128m); RF 362 feet (110.3m)
Turf: Grass (1910); Artificial Infield (1969); Grass Infield (1976)

New Comiskey Park
Chicago, IL
333 West 35th Street,
Chicago, IL 60616
(312) 831-1SOX
Home Team: Chicago White Sox
Opening Date: April 18, 1991
Capacity: 44,321
Outfield Dimensions: LF 347 feet (105.8m); CF 400 feet (121.9m); RF 347 feet (105.8m)
Turf: Bluegrass

Wrigley Field
Chicago, IL
1060 West Addison Street,
Chicago, IL 606132
(773) 404-CUBS
Home Team: Chicago Cubs
Opening Date: April 23, 1914
Capacity (Original; Latest): 14,000 (1914); 38,902 (1998)
Outfield Dimensions: LF 355 feet (108.2m); CF 400 feet (121.9m); RF 353 feet (107.6m)
Turf: Merion Bluegrass and clover

Maryland

Oriole Park at Camden Yards
Baltimore, MD
333 West Camden Street,
Baltimore, MD 21201
(401) 685-9800
Home Team: Baltimore Orioles
Opening Date: April 6, 1992
Capacity: 48,262
Outfield Dimensions: LF 333 feet (101.5m); CF 400 feet (121.9m); RF 318 feet (96.9m)
Turf: Maryland Bluegrass

Massachusetts

Fenway Park
Boston, MA
4 Yawkey Way, Boston,
MA 02215-3496
(617) 267-1700
Home Team: Boston Red Sox
Opening Date: April 20, 1912
Capacity (Original; Latest): 58,000 (1923); 57,545 (1980)
Outfield Dimensions: LF 340 feet (103.6m); CF 440 feet (121.9m); RF 325 feet (97m)
Turf: Bluegrass

Michigan

Tiger Stadium
Detroit, MI
2121 Trumbull Avenue,
Detroit, MI 48216
(313) 963-2050
Home Team: Detroit Tigers
Opening Date: April 20, 1912
Last Game: September 27, 1999
Capacity (Original; Latest): 23,000 (1912); 52,416 (1936)
Outfield Dimensions: LF 340 feet (103.6m); CF 440 feet (134.1m); RF 325 feet (99.1m)
Turf: Merion Bluegrass

Minnesota

Hubert H. Humphrey Metrodome
Minneapolis, MN
34 Kirby Puckett Place,
Minneapolis, MN 55415
(612) 375-1116 or (800) 33-TWINS
Home Team: Minnesota Twins
Opening Date: April 3, 1982
Capacity: 55,883
Outfield Dimensions: LF 344 feet (104.9m); CF 408 feet (124.4m); RF 327 feet (99.7m)
Turf: Astroturf

Missouri

Kauffman Stadium
Kansas City, MO
1 Royal Way, Kansas City, MO 64129
(816) 921-2200
Home Team: Kansas City Royals
Opening Date: April 10, 1973
Capacity: 40,625
Outfield Dimensions: LF 330 feet (100.6m); CF 410 feet (124.9m); RF 330 feet (100.6m)
Turf: Astroturf (1973); Grass (1995)

Busch Stadium
St. Louis, MO
250 Stadium Plaza,
St. Louis, MO 63102
(314) 421-3060
Home Team: St. Louis Cardinals
Opening Date: May 12, 1966
Capacity: 49,676
Outfield Dimensions: LF 330 feet (100.6m); CF 402 feet (122.5m); RF 330 feet (100.6m)
Turf: Grass (1966); Artificial (1970); Grass (1996)

New York

Yankee Stadium
Bronx, NY
E. 161st Street,
Bronx, NY 10451
(718) 293-6000
Home Team: New York Yankees
Opening Date: April 18, 1923
Capacity (Original; Latest): 58,000 (1923); 57,545 (1980)
Outfield Dimensions: LF 318 feet (96.9m); CF 408 feet (124.4m); RF 314 feet (95.7m)
Turf: Merion Bluegrass

Ebbets Field
Brooklyn, NY
Home Team: Brooklyn Dodgers
Opening Date: April 9, 1913
Last Game: September 24, 1957
Capacity (Original; Latest): 25,000 (1913); 32,000 (1932)
Outfield Dimensions: LF 419 feet (106.1m); CF 450 feet (122m); RF 301 feet (107.6m)
Turf: Grass

Shea Stadium
Flushing, NY
123-01 Roosevelt Avenue,
Flushing, NY 11368
(718) 507-METS; Tickets (718) 507-TIXX
Home Team: New York Mets
Opening Date: April 17, 1964
Capacity: 55,601
Outfield Dimensions: LF 338 feet (103m); CF 410 feet (125m); RF 338 feet (103m)
Turf: Bluegrass

Polo Grounds (IV)
New York, NY
Home Teams: New York Giants 1911–57; New York Yankees 1913–22; New York Mets 1962–63
Opening Date: June 28, 1911
Last Game: September 18, 1963
Capacity (Original; Latest): 34,000 (1911); 55,000 (1923)
Outfield Dimensions: LF 279 feet (85m); CF 483 feet (147.2m); RF 257 feet (78.3m)
Turf: Grass

Ohio

Cinergy Field
Cincinnati, OH
100 Cinergy Field,
Cincinnati, OH 45202
(513) 421-4510
Home Team: Cincinnati Reds
Opening Date: June 30, 1970
Capacity: 52,952
Outfield Dimensions: LF 330 feet (100.6m); CF 404 feet (123.1m); RF 330 feet (100.6m)
Turf: Astroturf 8

Jacobs Field
Cleveland, OH
2401 Ontario Street,
Cleveland, OH 44115
(216) 420-4200
Home Team: Cleveland Indians
Opening Date: April 4, 1994
Capacity: 43,345
Outfield Dimensions: LF 325 feet (99.1m); CF 405 feet (123.4m); RF 325 feet (99.1m)
Turf: Kentucky Bluegrass

Ontario

SkyDome
Toronto, Ontario
One Blue Jays Way,
Toronto, Ontario M5V 1J1
(416) 341-1234 or (888) 654-6528
Home Team: Toronto Blue Jays
Opening Date: June 5, 1989
Capacity: 50,516
Outfield Dimensions: LF 328 feet (100m); CF 400 feet (121.9m); RF 328 feet (99.9m)
Turf: Astroturf

Pennsylvania

Veterans Stadium
Philadelphia, PA
3501 South Broad Street,
Philadelphia, PA 19148
(215) 463-1000
Home Team: Philadelphia Phillies
Opening Date: April 4, 1971
Capacity: 62,382
Outfield Dimensions: LF 330 feet (100.6m); CF 408 feet (124.4m); RF 330 feet (100.6m)
Turf: Astroturf

Three Rivers Stadium
Pittsburgh, PA
600 Stadium Circle,
Pittsburgh, PA 15212
(412) 321-2827 or (800) 289-2827
Home Team: Pittsburgh Pirates
Opening Date: July 16, 1970
Capacity: 47,971
Outfield Dimensions: LF 335 feet (102.1m); CF 400 feet (121.9m); RF 335 feet (102.1m)
Turf: Tartanturf (1970); Astroturf (1983)

Quebec

Olympic Stadium
Montreal, Quebec
4549 Pierre de Coubertin,
Montreal, Quebec H1V3N7
(514) 253-3434
Home Team: Montreal Expos
First Expos game: April 15, 1977
Capacity: 46,500
Outfield Dimensions: LF 325 feet (99.1m); CF 404 feet (123.1m); RF 325 feet (99.1m)
Turf: Astroturf

Texas

The Ballpark in Arlington
Arlington, TX
100 Ballpark Way,
Arlington, TX 76011
(817) 273-5222; Tickets (817) 273-5000
Home Team: Texas Rangers
Opening Date: April 1, 1994
Capacity: 49,178
Outfield Dimensions: LF 334 feet (101.8m); CF 400 feet (121.9m); RF 325 feet (99.1m)
Turf: Tifway 419 Bermuda Grass

Astrodome
Houston, TX
8400 Kirby Drive,
Houston, TX 77054
(713) 799-9500
Home Team: Houston Astros
Opening Date: April 12, 1965
Capacity (Original; Latest): 42,217 (1965); 54,816 (1990)
Outfield Dimensions: LF 325 feet (99.1m); CF 400 feet (121.9m); RF 325 feet (99.1m)
Turf: Tifway 419 Bermuda Grass (1965); Astroturf (1966)

Washington

SAFECO Field
Seattle, WA
83 King Street, Seattle, WA 98104
(206) 346-4000; Tickets (206) 622-HITS
Home Team: Seattle Mariners
Opening Date: July 15, 1999
Capacity: 46, 621
Outfield Dimensions: LF 331 feet (100.9m); CF 405 feet (123.4m); RF 326 feet (99.4m)
Turf: Grass

Wisconsin

Milwaukee County Stadium
Milwaukee, WI
201 South 46th Street,
Milwaukee, WI 53201
(800) 933-7890 or (414) 933-9000
Home Team: Milwaukee Brewers
Opening Date: April 6, 1953
Capacity (Original; Latest): 36,011 (1953); 53,192 (1975)
Outfield Dimensions: LF 315 feet (96m); CF 402 feet (122.5m); RF 315 feet (96m)
Turf: Bluegrass

SELECTED BIBLIOGRAPHY

Adams, Bruce, and Margaret Engel. *Ballpark Vacations: Great Family Trips to Minor League and Classic Major League Baseball Parks Across America.* New York: Fodor's Travel Publications, 1997.

Ahuja, Jay. *Fields of Dreams: A Guide to Visiting and Enjoying All 30 Major League Ballparks.* Secaucus, N.J.: Citadel Press, 1998.

Benson, Michael. *Ballparks of North America: A Comprehensive Historical Reference to Baseball Grounds, Yards and Stadiums, 1845 to Present.* Jefferson, N.C.: McFarland and Company, 1989.

Chadwick, Bruce, and David M. Spindel. *The Giants: Memories and Memorabilia from a Century of Baseball.* New York: Abbeville Press, 1993.

Gershman, Michael. *Diamonds: The Evolution of the Ballpark.* Boston: Houghton Mifflin Company, 1993.

Lowry, Philip J. *Green Cathedrals: The Ultimate Celebration of All 273 Major League and Negro League Ballparks Past and Present.* Reading, Mass.: Addison Wesley Publishing Co. 1992.

Palacios, Oscar, and Eric Robin. *Ballpark Sourcebook: Diamond Diagrams.* Skokie, Ill.: STATS Publishing, 1998.

Reidenbaugh, Lowell. *The Sporting News: Take Me Out to the Ballpark.* St. Louis: Sporting New Publishing Co., 1983.

Ritter, Lawrence S. *Lost Ballparks: A Celebration of Baseball's Legendary Fields.* New York: Penguin Studio Books, 1992.

Tackach, James, and Joshua B. Stein. *The Fields of Summer: America's Great Ballparks and the Players Who Triumphed in Them.* New York: Crescent Books, 1992.

Ward, Geoffrey C., and Ken Burns. *Baseball: An Illustrated History*. New York: Alfred A. Knopf, 1994.

Wood, Bob. *Dodger Dogs to Fenway Franks: The Ultimate Guide to America's Top Baseball Parks.* New York: McGraw Hill, 1988.

PHOTO CREDITS

© Russ Andorka, p. 106

© Brian Bahr/AllSport USA, p. 92; © Tim Brokema/AllSport USA, p. 46; © Otto Greule Jr./AllSport USA, pp. 58 left, 59; © Jonathan Daniel/AllSport USA, pp. 19 bottom, 27 top, 47 center, 112; © Stephen Dunn/AllSport USA, pp. 18–19, 94–95, 96 top, 97, 104 right; © Tom Hauck/AllSport USA, p. 15; © Jeff Hixon/AllSport USA, p. 69 bottom; © Vincent LaForet/AllSport USA, pp. 20–21; © Zoran Milich/AllSport USA, pp. 52, 54; © Don Smith/ AllSport USA, pp. 16–17; © Rick Stewart/AllSport USA, pp. 55, 93 bottom; Matthew Stockman/ AllSport USA, pp. 66–67

AP/Wide World Photos, pp. 30–31, 42–43

Chris Bain Collection, pp. 33 bottom, 75 top right, endpapers

Baseball Hall of Fame Library Cooperstown, N.Y., pp. 14 bottom, 24, 30, 36, 56, 61, 80 bottom, 85 bottom, 68, 70 bottom, 73 bottom, 75 top left, 78 top, 79, 87 top, 87 bottom, 88 top, 93 top left, 98, 109 bottom;

©Jonathan Busser, p. 80 top

Corbis, pp. 40 bottom, 50 bottom; Corbis/AFP, pp. 95, 103 bottom, 104 top, 105; Corbis/Bettmann, pp. 8, 11, 14 top, 22, 25, 27 bottom, 39, 41 bottom, 44 left, 45, 48, 73 top, 73 center, 75 bottom right, 76 left, 76 right, 96 bottom; Corbis/Catherine Karnow, p. 60; Corbis/Neal Preston, p. 62 bottom; Corbis/ Reuters Newmedia Inc., pp. 70 right, 113; Corbis/Vince Streano, p. 63 top; Corbis/Ted Streshinsky, p. 57; Corbis/UPI, pp. 28 top, 44 right, 49 bottom left

© David Durochik, p. 109 top

FPG International, pp. 6–7, 38, 49 top; ©James Blank/FPG International, p. 71; ©Jerry Driendl/FPG International, p. 77 top; ©Peter Gridley/FPG International, pp. 12–13; ©Michael Hart/FPG International, p. 64; ©William Holmes/FPG International, p. 74; ©Jay Lurie/FPG International, p. 72; ©Gary Randall/FPG International, pp. 90–91; Michael Tamborrino/FPG International, p. 51 bottom

© Mark Hicks, p. 37

Index Stock, pp. 78–79

© Tim Jackson, pp. 82, 100

©Thomason Productions/Leo de Wys Inc., p. 65 top

© Thomas H. Mitchell/New England Stock Photo, p. 40 top; © Jim Schwabel/New England Stock Photo, p. 69 top

MRB Images, Inc., pp. 89, 98–99

Kathryn Siegler, pp. 1–2, 108, 110, 111

SportsChrome East/West, p. 88 bottom; © Rob Tringali/ SportsChrome USA, pp. 2–3, 51 top, 62 top, 90; © Scott Troyanos/SportsChrome USA, pp. 102, 103 top

© David Spindel, pp. 10, 28 center, 33 top, 34, 38 left, 41 top, 43, 47 top, 50 top, 58 left, 63 bottom, 65 bottom, 68, 70 bottom, 73 bottom, 75 top left, 78 top, 79, 87 top, 87 bottom, 88 top, 93 top left, 98, 109 bottom; David Spindel Collection, pp. 28 bottom left, 47 bottom, 49 bottom right, 77 bottom, endpapers

Sports Imagery, p. 32; © Gene Boyars/Sports Imagery, pp. 26–27, 34–35

© Peter Zay/Transparencies, Inc, p. 81

© Bernard Boutrit/Woodfin Camp & Associates, p. 19 top

Unicorn Stock Photos/ChromaSohn, p. 29

Every effort has been made to ascertain and correctly credit the copyright holders and/or owners for all images appearing in this book. The publisher will correct mistaken credits and include any omitted credits in all future editions.

INDEX